Collusion

ALSO BY EVAN ZIMROTH

novel
Gangsters

poetry
Dead, Dinner, or Naked
Giselle Considers Her Future

Collusion

Memoir of a Young Girl and Her Ballet Master

Evan Zimroth

HarperFlamingo

An Imprint of HarperCollins*Publishers*

HarperCollins books may be purchased for educational, business, or sales promotional use. For information please write: Special Markets Department, HarperCollins Publishers, Inc., 10 East 53rd Street, New York, NY 10022.

FIRST EDITION

Designed by Kyoko Watanabe

Library of Congress Cataloging-in-Publication Data

Zimroth, Evan, 1943–
Collusion: memoir of a young girl and her ballet master /
Evan Zimroth. — 1st ed.
p.   cm.
ISBN 0-06-018786-7
I. Title.
PS3576.I516C6   1998
813'.54—dc21   98-16830

99 00 01 02 03 ❖/RRD 10 9 8 7 6 5 4 3 2 1

For my father,
and in memory of my mother

Contents

Acknowledgments

I wish to thank my editor, Terry Karten, for her vision and experience: Her acute intuitiveness and sweet persistence on behalf of *Collusion* helped me immeasurably. I am happily indebted also to Lydia Wills, my agent, who gave me courage to begin this memoir and was with me every step of the way. My family, then and now, sustained me generously, as only the best families do. I am very grateful to all of them, and especially to my daughters, Lilly and Kate, who encourage me daily, offer excellent literary advice, and keep me anchored in real life. I am also more than ever aware of my good fortune in having friends like Diane Steiner, B.J. Lunin-Frishberg, and Ed Marston, who have known me for years and who have lifted my spirits (as always) with the right word at the right time.

It makes me especially happy to record a loving thank-you to Judi Witt Fried, who was there from the beginning, who shared her memories with me, and who at the start of this book gave me the gold charm that I wear on a necklace, as I used to wear my long-ago ballerina.

Prelude

"Did it hurt?"
No, I lied.
"Do you want it again?"
Yes, I lied again.

$\mathcal{I}$ had just been raped, or so I told myself. But rape was not quite what had happened: Even at that moment of fear and panic and anger when he grabbed me, pinned me to the bed, and pressed himself into me, I knew you couldn't really call it rape. For one thing, I was "in love" with him. For another, we were in a motel, somewhere in the Blue Ridge Mountains, although exactly where we lodged I could not have said; it might have been Virginia, West Virginia, Tennessee, or the moon for all I cared. The day had been wonderful—we had driven lazily through the mountains, stopping at one Civil War battlefield after another to read their impressive Latinate signs, telling us who fought what battle where and under what dire circumstances. At least he said the inscriptions were Latinate, and read them aloud to me with much pleasure. I, as usual, felt too young, embarrassingly uneducated, and resolved that when I got back to college and could sign up for my spring semester courses, I would start Latin. How had I missed Latin when it would turn out to be so important for reading Civil War battlefield inscriptions in this, my first real love affair?

After the battlefields we had stopped in some small, depressed southern town in the mountains to find dinner and a motel. The meal was enchanting, despite the unpalatable food; the waiter had even found us a bottle of wine, although it was clear that the restaurant did not often serve it. My companion fingered the stem of his wineglass in a gesture that would become meaningful, and ominous, for me in the years that this affair wore on. It meant sex; it meant, *Later I will fuck you, and let's have none of your nonsense. Later we'll make love, whether you want it or not.*

Why did the sex turn out to be so awful? Why was I so reluctant? Why couldn't I just give in, let go, open up, enjoy it? Why did I suddenly find myself fighting and struggling to push away the man I was in love with—this man whom I had thought about constantly for months, wondering when I would see him again, when he would call me, wondering whether he was as overwhelmed as I was by the sheer presence of the other? When he had telephoned me in my dormitory room at college for a dinner date, I had gotten sick at the sound of his voice, faint and dizzy from wanting him so badly. So why was I fighting him off in some lost motel room deep in the Blue Ridge Mountains?

He did, very sensibly, what many men would have done in the circumstances: He decided that the struggle was part of my naive courtship, that I "really wanted it," pinned me down, and took me. For me, it was the first time. Afterward I lay in his arms, so glad it was over, laughing and crying, deeply in love with him and overcome with exhaustion, guilty at what I had forced him to do. I seemed to be bleeding ever so slightly. "Help," I cried tremuluously, throwing my arms around him. "I've been raped." "Yes, I suppose you have," he answered, gently kissing me. "Did it hurt? Do you want it again?"

The questions were oddly familiar. For a moment I tried to place them, and then with a sudden burst of memory I knew where I had heard that exact questioning before. I had been twelve, and had just been struck by F., my ballet master. For the first time. In fact the violence had been meted out with a leather cane on the very day I entered F.'s class, the Advanced Class, as punishment—or so I thought—for my still inexperienced and inexact classical technique.

As in the motel room where I was introduced to the dark strangeness of love, the violence in the ballet classroom was also an initiation. There, too, a man had taken me, possessed me, and launched me into a new world with one swift and indelible act. The questions in the motel room, with their echo from the past, overwhelmed me with knowledge I had never spoken of and had tried not to think of for years. The repetition of the questions showed me that F., too, although he had been my ballet master and I only a young student aspiring to a life as a dancer, had initiated me into another story. A love story. That realization, just as much as F.'s first act of violence, left me stunned.

The day I entered F.'s class, even though I had just become an Advanced student, I was still dressed like a little girl in the ballet uniform of the school—black cotton leotard, soft pink ballet slippers, white socks turned down at the ankle. I looked like all the little girls seen in old photographs of the Bolshoi or the Kirov, girls who have a certain exquisite air of innocence because they have not yet been allowed to graduate from white socks to pink tights. I stood at the barre doing my *demi-pliés*, my *grandes-pliés* in the five positions, and had just started the slight stretching and pointing exercise called *battement tendu*, when F. began one of his usual perambulations around the class, passing student by student, whistling at the top of his lungs, and pausing every now and again to make a slight adjustment in someone's placement.

When he came to me, he stopped at my side and looked me over. As far as I knew, he had noticed me only once before, briefly, on the day that he had dropped into my Intermediate lesson and had invited me into his Advanced Class. Where I had wanted to be, more than anywhere. "Straighten your leg," he now directed me quietly. I did so, of course, not looking at him at all but staring ahead as I had been taught and continuing with my assigned *tendus*.

"Straighten your leg," he repeated, and again I did so, trying harder, wondering about myself because it seemed to me that my leg was as straight as I could possibly make it. But when I extended my leg out to the side, as straight and taut and "pulled up" as I could manage, F. suddenly and without warning raised his cane and struck me across the inside of my thigh. I could hear it coming down. The cane left a long, thin, red mark.

I lost my breath in pain and amazement, lost my balance, and fell back against the barre. So this was Advanced Class, this was being a dancer! F. looked at me politely, sardonically. "Did it hurt?" he inquired.

Yes, sir.

"Do you want it again?"

No, sir.

"Then keep your leg straight in *battements tendus*," he said, and whistling cheerfully he continued his progress around the studio. Righting myself, I finished the exercise with my classmates and turned around at the barre to start again on the other side.

*   *   *

The first time F. struck me I felt as if I had been violated in the most private, secret way, even though the act took place, flagrant and unhidden, in the classroom. Perhaps because he hit the inner part of my thigh, where I was naked, perhaps because F. made it clear that he could do it again, perhaps because unwittingly I looked into F.'s eyes and saw there his satisfaction, I became dizzy with shock. And I said nothing, nothing at all except the words F. wanted to hear. Not only had I not raised a hand or said a word to defend myself, I felt as if I had entered into a secret alliance with him, a bond that could (and would) be cemented again and again. Although the word itself— "rape"—did not come to mind, I knew that a line had been crossed. By both of us. I had been taken— violated—not in the criminal way of terror and police reports, but in the old-fashioned, swooning way of the romance novel.

Violence is intimate, I know now, no matter that it is delivered publicly, in front of your classmates, as it was that day with F. It divides you against yourself and scrambles your impulses. Your synapses are immediately overloaded, overcharged; you short out. Later you writhe at the memory; you cannot believe you were so febrile. So willing. But I was; I acquiesced.

Once I regained my equilibrium and my brain cells

quieted down from their whirling, I marveled at my initiation into this new world of artistic devotion, where the body seems infinitely malleable and the purity of one's line is worth any cost. The swift, precise cruelty, the catechism of questions, the mark on my body: I had been baptized into a new realm. I was even grateful.

With that swift flash of violence, the ballet exercises had a new meaning; in fact, the world itself seemed different, more pregnant with possibility. The simplest, most basic movements of the body in the prescribed forms of classical ballet had suddenly a new efficacy—they were potentially beautiful, potentially perfect. They could make someone watch and admire. My body could make even the revered F. halt his apparently casual strolls around the class to shine on me the spotlight of his unquestioned authority, to warm me with some potent mix of unfathomable threat and artistry and cherishing. After that one brutal stroke—and my acquiescence—whenever F. walked toward me or touched me, the quality of the air around me changed.

It took romance in a seedy motel room in the Blue Ridge Mountains for me to hear the echo of F.'s words as a lover's litany. *Did it hurt? Do you want it again?* Yes, and yes. The man wanted it again, too; in fact, they both wanted it again, the lover and F. Now I see that. Now I see that the violence in both cases wasn't random, nor was it—for F.—a desire only to punish me. It was a question, an epistemology, a way to find something out. They were searching not so much for evidence of the pain they inflicted but for what I might memorably give at their request: my surrender.

When F. first so unexpectedly hit me, he taught me more than to pay attention to the small things, like *battement tendu*. He also showed me beyond words what it felt like to be a woman, with a woman's submission and a woman's power over a man. I see now that I did not in the ordinary sense "grow up": I was a child, and then one stunning moment later I was a woman; I felt the change immediately. I moved beyond childhood in the instant of discovering something I could not have possibly known before—that I could submit to the violence of love, recognize it as love, and be complicit in it. It wasn't the pain that propelled me into awareness; pain up to a certain point is neutral, especially for dancers. It was the mark on my flesh, the look in F.'s eyes.

How did I "become" a woman? Certainly not in any biological sense. Nothing outward changed. With the rest of my class, I continued as if nothing had happened. But I felt as if the universe had shifted around me. Before F. struck me I was just a little girl doing her ballet exercises at the barre, routinely, because I wanted to dance and was expected to do these exercises daily, without fail. Every dancer does so, from the youngest beginner to the most renowned prima ballerina.

"Do you want to be a great dancer?" F. had once asked me before admitting me to his Advanced Class, asking with evident irony because he was talking to a twelve-year-old child. But there was nothing I wanted more, no sacrifice too great for such an ideal. I would be Plisetskaya, I would be Pavlova, Spessivtzeva, Ulanova: My insignificant little *battements tendus* were the beginning, the promise, of a future of exhilarating mastery. F. moved me, in one instant, from the innocent ballet dreams of my childhood to the demands of a possible ballet career with its adult transactions of reciprocal power, ambiguous cruelty, restless ambition.

Of course, we were all young dancers, forming ourselves, imperfect, far, far from adept at ballet technique. But F. when he struck me singled me out from the others and made me his own, his possession. In ballet language, ballet code, F.'s stinging cruelty announced that he desired me, desired my body, would take and mold it because I was his favorite one, pliable and promising. Even beautiful. Because I was his treasured one, I would gradually embody for him his vision of artistry, of ballet perfection: He would limn that vision on *my* body, day after day in ballet class, giving me strength, technique, a beautiful "line," musicality, and the kind of passionate lyricism that can be taught by only the rarest of gifted teachers. I never

wanted it otherwise. His act was both almost rhapsodic and yet deeply controlled—"proper" is the only
word for it—an act that left me breathless and taken.
The mark he left on my inner thigh was a brand, my
initiation into ownership. It changed me utterly. I
knew I would be marked by him forever.

And yet . . . There was another story beyond our
shared devotion to artistry and the joy of devoting
oneself, body and soul, to the ideals of classical technique. That story stems from some simple facts: F.
struck me. Repeatedly. I didn't object. On the contrary, I became more and more in thrall to F.'s violence—always delivered as it was that first time in a
quiet, orderly, ritualized way—his strange punishments for technical lapses, the insults and carefully
calibrated humiliation. Ballet is a world in which
"normal" values are reversed: Brutality is seen as a gift,
fear as devotion, sadism as love.

These experiences, no matter how painful, never
felt to me like child abuse, just as I knew in the motel
room that even though I struggled and was bleeding, I
hadn't—quite—been raped. The truth was that I
adored F., much more than I have ever allowed myself
to adore anyone since. Therefore I allowed him to do
whatever he wanted with me, to me, in the interest of
artistic devotion: Such was the tacit bargain we
enacted, a bargain in which I was completely complicit. Devotion to the art of ballet became devotion to

F. and his erotic power over me, thwarted and laced with irony as it was. My own growing sexuality was entangled with ambition, with pleasing him, and with the pleasure of my own power over him as well.

I wish I could know now, at this moment, whether the relationship was erotic for F., too. Everything that I know about him suggests how much he needed women: that he surrounded himself with women, that he married younger and younger dancers, that he groomed young women, keeping them attached to him, anxious and adoring. There was always a chain of dancers revolving around him doing his bidding, as if he were the Sun King and we were all courtiers or acolytes. He would bestow attention—sometimes brutally—and then become moody and distant, unreachable. Even his wife couldn't reach him but respectfully kept her distance, as if for her own protection. What we all shared, I think, was the awareness that his attention could always be withdrawn, that there was always someone else waiting to claim it—someone younger, thinner, more beautiful, more promising, a better dancer.

So when F. favored me, picked me out of the crowd, and welcomed me to Advanced Class with his stroke of violence, when he groomed me to reach heights of technical artistry I had only dreamed of, it had to have been erotic for him. Or so I think. The violence itself had a sexual rhythm: the anticipation, the quick strike, the withdrawal into impersonality, almost anonymity, afterward. When I heard through the dancers' grapevine that another ballet teacher had been arrested for pedophilia I wasn't the least surprised. F. never quite took that risk, although I imagined for years that he might. I wished for it. So if the experience with me wasn't erotic for him, I am sorry. Truly sorry. I did everything I could to make it so.

Because F. has saturated my consciousness for so long—appearing in dreams, stories, chance encounters, my real and my fantasy life—it was inevitable that one day I would write about him. I started that process long ago, by writing down some of the vignettes that are now part of the fabric of *Collusion*. Once, in an unguarded moment, I took out these stories and asked a friend to read them. I watched while he read: With every page he shook his head no, no, no, back and forth. When he was finished he handed back the sheaf of papers as if I had passed him gasoline and a match. "Put these away," he said. "Your children should never see them."

But I knew that I would continue writing about F., about how I came to him and why, how he took me and changed not only my body but transformed some essential part of me, and how, in the end, it was necessary that I leave him. Although any dancer (any female dancer, that is) would immediately comprehend the nature of my relationship to F. and could substitute her *own* F.—the revered teacher who strikes fear in her heart all the while imparting the most valuable gifts—my children will, I hope, understand that I am writing only one person's story of life in the hothouse world of ballet, not a paradigm for living.

But it is hard, harder than I had ever realized, to write about my love for F. with its strange cruelties and silences, to confess that I took part freely, it was my fault, I liked it, I wanted it; in fact I sought it out and submitted to it again and again. To confess that, at barely thirteen, I enjoyed the subtle eroticism of power, the delicate interplay of threat and surrender, of one person's possession, unquestioned, of another. My closed world of ballet school, or so it might seem to the outsider (although never to me), was like one of those child-sex rings we are all so appalled to discover existing under our very eyes, with that talented scoutmaster, that grandfather so devoted to young children, that priest, that charismatic director of a children's theater group. That ballet master.

Someone else, a "real person" (even today I make this distinction), would want me to see that my acquiescence, my continuing surrender, was wrong, that I hurt myself, that I allowed someone else to hurt me. Or perhaps to see that I had no choice, that I was a child preyed on by an adult. Both possibilities depress me, sensible as they are about what to me has always been private, secret, obsessive. I knew then, in my childhood, and continue to believe now that I was not a hostage to F.'s violence. Mutually, reciprocally, we had struck a covenant of possession, the mark on my body a symbol of alliance between a young dancer and the ballet master she adored.

Even now, if I could choose, I would live my connection to F. all over again. I don't want to be free of the memories; I am not looking to be redeemed by them. They have a claim on me that is more powerful than sex or love or food, as if my long-ago surrender to F. forever altered the structure of my chromosomes.

Children can collude. I colluded. I loved him.

Part 1

~ The Body Never Forgets

Brisées, legs beating, then *brisées volées*, the same beats but flying through the air—I love these!—beats alternating left and right, then a string of *sauts de basque* ("Doubles, please. If you can"), then *grands jetés* on the diagonal, from one corner of the studio to the other, as fast as we can, faster, our legs scissoring apart, splits in the air, all of us leaping one after another with the velocity of racehorses coursing to the finish. "Speed, girls, speed—but low, keep it low. Speed, not height. Faster, faster! Keep it moving." Our teacher, Sonya, circles the room, jumping out of our way when she has to, directing traffic with both hands, an unlit cigarette in one of them. "*Left* side passes in front. Keep your eyes *open*, girls!"—she has to shout over Mr. Shurbanov's pounding piano chords—"No crashes, please! *Travel*, ladies, travel. Keep it going!" Then: *piqué* turns sharp and fast, on the diagonal, fast whirling steps, dizzying. Sonya snaps her fingers for each beat, each turn; our heads snap, too. "Spot, girls! *Spot!* Don't lose it." If we can catch a few seconds, we drop into a half crouch, almost doubled over with hands on our knees like football players, panting and gulping air, heads raised to fill our lungs. The air is thick and salty with our sweat.

Somewhere in all the spinning and leaping, F. has quietly entered the studio. He walks in on exaggerated tiptoe as if he means to be invisible, and lowers himself, lithe as a cat, onto a bench in front of the mirror. Sonya is still circling the class, pretending to ignore him—she can do that; she's his wife—but we ballet girls are instantly ignited. We spring up in the air with renewed energy and *ballon* because now we have a visitor, an audience, the great teacher who is more godlike to us than real. Sonya doesn't need to urge us on; we *travel*.

F. is legendary: We tell stories about him constantly, but I have hardly ever caught a glimpse of him before. Since I am twelve and only an Intermediate, he has always been remote, beyond my sphere, almost a mirage. From the time I had first come to his school, we ballet girls had posted ourselves outside the closed door of his classes listening to him whistle along with the piano as his Advanced students practiced. We listened to the silences in between the bursts of music, when, as we imagined, F. was inspiring his dancers to accomplish more, admonishing them for their mistakes, creating new and intricate combinations for them to dance. When class was over, F. would open the door, turn back toward his class and give his students a sardonic little nonchalant bow—just the slightest hint of one—while the dancers applauded. I already knew that it was traditional for dancers to applaud at the end of each class (usually perfunctorily), but I loved F.'s self-effacing mockery as he acknowledged the tribute—not ever completely ignoring it but not basking in it either, one hand on the doorknob so that he could make a quick exit. Then he would disappear into his office while his dancers trooped out behind him, exhausted and exhilarated, dripping wet, with their towels thrown casually around their necks. When we entered the studio for our own class, the huge mirror covering one wall would still be blurred with steam from their sweat.

But today—no fireworks from F., no displays, no sardonic bows. Rather disappointingly F. just sits immobile and stares at us, his wiry, lithe body folded together, knees crossed, elbow on knee, and head in hand. He looks glum. He has a hooked nose, I notice, and intense, brooding eyes that measure us, as if he were calculating when to uncoil himself and spring.

"All together," Sonya calls out, banging with her hand on the barre until Mr. Shurbanov looks up from where he is hunched over the piano keys, obliviously pounding out chords. A cigarette smolders away untouched in an ashtray several octaves above middle

C. Okay, okay, he finally nods, finishing with a flourish of notes. "Places, please," Sonya says. At her direction, we all move to our assigned places in the class, standing in fifth position like little marionettes and filling up the studio with our neat rows. "*Sous-sous*, *entrechat-quatre* four times; seven *changements*"—we hear the beat already—"last one, *entrechat*. Left side." We do this once, twice, pausing only for a quick reminder about *épaulement*, the tilt of our shoulders, while we gasp for air, then again, once, twice. But we dance our hearts out—F. is watching. He doesn't move, but his eyes dart around sharply. Each of us is hoping he is watching her.

Class is over: We curtsy and head for the door when F. half straightens up and with short blasts of whistling beckons me over to him, waving his arms like a traffic cop. He still looks dour. Gazing at me intently, he examines me from head to toe while I stand stock still in front of him, apprehensive about why he called me over and still beet red from the exertions of class. He studies me as if I were a little morsel of mouse and he a coiled snake, ready to dart and devour. I want to wipe the sweat from my face but am afraid to move.

"Do you want to be a great dancer?" he asks finally with quiet sarcasm, cocking his head, as if the inappropriateness of asking this question of a twelve-year old amuses him. Sonya, now sitting next to him on the bench and still a little winded herself, gives him a sudden startled look. Despite F.'s ironic demeanor, his question comes at me like an electric shock. The formulation "great dancer" has never occurred to me before: the utter, intense visionary quality of the idea. I want to dance, I love my lessons, but—a great dancer?

"Yes," I say immediately, as if I know what it means.

F. turns to his wife and mumbles something incomprehensible under his breath. She seems to agree, and then they both look up and motion to me that I can go. As I reach the door, Sonya calls out to me, as if it were an afterthought, "From now on you'll go to Advanced."

I turn around and see the two of them still sitting on the bench in front of the mirror, husband and wife, Sonya ignoring him once again to light her cigarette, and F. coiled up as tightly as before, chin in hand and staring at me dourly. I nod.

So that is F., and I am chosen! Once out of his sight I jump straight up in the air, whirl myself over to the water fountain for a great gulp of cold water, and *grand-jeté* down the hall toward the dressing room.

First I had to find Astrid, my confidante and Beginners Class teacher, whom I had loved from the moment she had walked into our class and introduced herself to us in her sweet, high-pitched voice. She was where I thought she would be, in her private dressing room, looking at herself in the mirror and sticking hairpins into her dancer's bun. Sliding onto the bench next to her, I told her I needed to talk. It was too embarrassing to announce that I was going to be a great dancer but I told her everything else, how F. had scrutinized me, how afraid I had been to move, how Sonya had said, ". . . you'll go to Advanced."

Astrid's eyes sparkled at me in the mirror. "That's wonderful!" she said. "You'll have F. now. Every day, Studio One, at four-thirty."

"But I like *Sonya*!" I found myself wailing to my great surprise, because in fact I did not like Sonya at all and had repeatedly imagined what it would be like to "have" F., to be on the inside of that studio applauding with the other Advanced dancers after an exhilarating class while our ballet master headed out the door with his insolent, self-conscious mimicry of a bow.

"Don't worry, you'll love F.," Astrid assured me. "He gives a great class. You just have to get used to him, that's all."

How one might get used to a self-mocking, ironic, dapper, and demanding ballet instructor, always impeccably dressed in loose trousers, white shirt and bow tie, who ended his class as coolly as he began it, whistling nonchalantly as if the universe itself were attuned to his melodies, I had no idea. *He* was the one who opened the door at the end of class, I suddenly realized; everyone else was captive inside until he left. What if I needed to escape? What if I weren't good enough? What if he didn't like me? Would he throw me out? Demote me?

Astrid didn't answer. Then, swiftly, while I watched her in the mirror, she reached around to the back of her neck and unhooked her necklace. I remember intently watching her face in the mirror as she unclasped the chain with its dangling silver talisman, a toy ballerina, the kind one sees revolving inside a jewelry box to the tinkly sounds of *Swan Lake*. Then, catching my own reflection in the mirror, I watched as Astrid fastened her necklace around my neck. It enchanted me almost to tears, that miniature ballerina in the hollow of my throat, poised on one silvery toe in perpetual arabesque. Full of gratitude for Astrid's gesture and now linked to her forever through her gift, I wore the ballerina charm always, never once taking it off until I stopped dancing entirely. I felt as if I had been anointed.

Ballet is not real life; they are two separate realms. "Real life" is the phrase dancers use to mean the life that is foreclosed to them—ordinary, banal life in which real people go about their commonplace business, eating three meals a day and indulging their random enthusiasms without the dancer's bracing devotion to daily ballet class. In ballet, on the other hand, the routines of real life are willingly, devotionally replaced by the dancer's fervor for artistry, the dancer's allegiance to the liturgies of classical technique.

Real life didn't matter to me; only ballet life had value. There F. would make me not only a dancer but a *great* dancer. He had promised.

By the time I was almost thirteen and in F.'s Advanced Class, I had already known from when I was a small child that I wanted to be a dancer. Even though I could have had no clear idea of what it meant to follow such a vocation, I knew I was destined for it and determined to move heaven and earth to achieve it. The simple act of placing my body for the first time at the ballet barre with my left hand lightly resting on the wood and my feet turned out in first position, ready to begin the most basic of ballet exercises, confirmed in me the dedication I had felt in myself since my early childhood.

But my life at first was not so different from the lives of countless other little girls—talented, naturally thin, happily ambitious little girls—who decide in their precocity that they must at all costs become ballet dancers. We are children of kind, liberal, endlessly beneficent parents who want us to be exposed to everything, parents who give us piano and violin lessons, ice-skating, interpretive dance, and Sunday

school, rarely expecting that any of these introduc-
tions will take, will stick, will become the driving,
unstoppable force in their daughters' lives.

But unlike many other little girls, I had a mother
who was my first baby-step ballet teacher. She herself
had once been a dancer, or at least an incipient dancer,
certainly as promising and talented in her childhood
efforts as I would become in mine. I vividly remember
a photograph of her taken when she was about ten: a
slender, leggy girl in a tutu and toe shoes, her long hair
pulled back behind her ears and tied up on each side
with a broad, white bow. She is smiling shyly at the
camera, her chin tucked down, and her eyes brimming
with pleasure at some feat she has just accomplished.
The story my mother told me when I found the photograph was that she had just performed "at Town Hall,"
wherever that was; I was too young to ask. Then she
showed me that in the same box as the photograph
there was also a dance program on heavy paper now
tanning with age, my mother's name in small black letters written across the middle, and then at the top in
larger letters the words "Town Hall" and the date,
blurred beyond recognition. Perhaps she had just been
part of a recital and danced a solo like "The Dragonfly"
or "The Dying Swan," as little ballet girls did in those
days, in imitation of Anna Pavlova. The photograph is
indelible in my memory: From the moment of seeing
it, I knew that my mother was not someone remote

from my childhood but that she herself had once been an enchanting little girl who wore hair ribbons and pointe shoes and loved to dance. By teaching me my first lessons, she linked us in our haphazard American way to the great European tradition of ballet dynasties, in which a dance heritage is passed down from one generation to the next, not only from teacher to pupil but often from the father to his daughter or son. Certainly I knew that she was bequeathing to me something ceremonious and beguilingly formal.

When my mother began my lessons, she pulled over a chair in the living room to use as a barre and showed me the five positions of the feet, the five positions of the arms, called *port de bras*, and a few basic steps. I much preferred my mother's "First position, *demi-plié*" to the children's interpretive dance class she had enrolled me in ("Now let's all be frogs and see how high we can jump!"), which I detested at once and quickly dropped. Because my parents themselves loved the ballet, and perhaps because my mother remembered that a small child could be enraptured as well, they took me to see a performance of *Giselle*, where suddenly the whole panorama of classical dance opened itself up to me, from the music of Adolphe Adam to the ghostly cemetery and pure *ballet blanc* of Act 2, in which the Wilis, the spirits of jilted maidens, dance in their long, gauzy, white-as-death tutus.

I was so struck by the mad scene, when Giselle kills

herself over Albrecht's betrayal, that during intermission I staggered up the aisle going dramatically insane in my party dress and black patent Mary Janes. At home I plunged an imaginary sword into my breast and swooned gracefully to the floor, my legs neatly tucked under me. I didn't want to be a jumping frog; I wanted to be the frail peasant Giselle, buoyantly innocent until Albrecht jilts her and she dies rapturously for love. I wanted to do what I later learned was *pas de cheval* with Albrecht, to learn mime so that in stage language I could say "I love you!" and "Let's all dance!" and "Hark! I hear someone coming!" But even if I were going mad at sword-point, I wanted order and beauty and the stylized disposal of the limbs. I asked for real lessons.

But I was too young; my mother said that no good ballet school would allow me to start when my body was not yet formed enough in its ligaments and musculature to begin rigorous formal training. Even worse, her interest in teaching me *port de bras* had long since waned. Still I wanted to dance. Even though I had not seen another ballet performance since that first *Giselle*, I knew that to dance like that—to create onstage a narrative of love and betrayal all through exquisite sequences of movement—to do that I needed to know *steps*. Basics. Whatever came after first and second position.

Finally, when I was in fifth grade, I sought out a

classmate named Joanie, a girl to whom I was drawn primarily because she had just started her own ballet lessons. While the other kids were on the blacktop playing kickball and jump rope, I persuaded Joanie to escape with me to "do ballet." She obligingly took me to a quiet spot on the playground at recess and showed me how to do *pas de chat*, my first step. There was a patch of grass softening our steps and a large, flowering, overhanging bush shielding us, giving us a secluded stage for our lesson. The bush I remember particularly because it kept us hidden; I can see it even now and remember the sense of safety and privacy we felt behind its screen. What Joanie was teaching me was private, special, a technical feat unknown to me before that moment, that first pleasurable *pas de chat*. Not a word about first position or fifth position or *demi-plié* or turning out your feet. Just *pas de chat* on the grass, and that was it. *Pas de chat* means "cat step"; it's a jump meant to mimic the light, prowling motion of a cat in the air, landing in a subtle, delicate pounce. *Pas de chat* was beautiful, amazing. I did hundreds of them that first hour, all the while knowing that soon—I had no idea how—I would take real ballet lessons and become a dancer.

"The body never forgets" is said inevitably by every ballet teacher in the world as he (or she) leaves a thin, red welt on one's arm or leg or hip for being mis-placed, literally out of line. And it's true: My body never forgot. I remember everything. I remember exactly how warm the studio was that day in June when my parents signed me up for the first session of my formal ballet classes. Because it was summer and I was only a Beginner, classes were more relaxed than they would ever be again. F.'s wife—I had not then met or even heard of F.—welcomed me at the door to the studio, led me to the barre with the other girls, and said she would be my teacher. "Sonya," she said, plac-ing my left hand lightly on the barre. Although such casualness is practically unheard of in the hierarchical world of ballet, we always called her only by her first name. We were allowed this informality possibly because our lessons took place in the vacation inter-lude of summer, but more likely—as I was to learn later—because the traditional name, "Madame F.," was reserved for F.'s ancient mother, herself a former ballerina, who sometimes taught the Advanced girls.

A small, dark woman with an amused grin, Sonya had a meticulous approach to teaching us that I wel-comed because it told me that at last I was doing something serious, *real ballet!*, with rules, laws, stan-dards completely absent from my long-ago class in interpretive dance. We didn't walk tall like a princess or jump like a frog; instead we did *pliés*, and when we were finished with one set we turned around at the barre and did the same *pliés* all over again. We didn't do *pas de chats* at all until the summer's end: Until then we weren't ready. There was a kind of happiness and sweetness in that class that I never again found, even though I, probably more than the other Beginner girls, went about learning the routines and exercises as if my life depended on them. I couldn't get enough.

From the very beginning I felt *chosen* for this vocation, even though I certainly hadn't been, not then. The warm, damp air in the studio, the summer light shimmering with motes of dust brushed up by our feet as we practiced, the haze and heat visible through the barely open studio windows, the moist air smelling of resin, sweat, and traffic, the feel of the smooth wooden barre under my hand as I worked, the rhythmic melodies of real music starting and stopping from the piano—all of it was a deep pleasure to me. I remember my leotard of heavy black cotton, and how quickly it became damp as I did the exercises at the barre. By the time class ended with eight *changements* and then eight *changements* again, I was slippery with sweat and my shapeless leotard clung to my underpants. I remember doing *ronds des jambes*, inside and outside, *en dedans* and *en dehors*, on the floor and *en l'air*, while Sonya held my wrist, smiled at me, and said that in the fall, if I wished to and wanted to work hard, I could go directly into Advanced Beginner and then Intermediate Class.

In the fall we became serious. I was "promoted"

ahead of my classmates, cycling through the sequence
—Advanced Beginner, Intermediate I, Intermediate
II—more quickly than others and never staying stationary in one class long enough to develop a best
friend. My teacher in those early classes was a young
dancer named Astrid Aalgard, still a student herself, a
diminutive girl with a cherubic face and a sweet, gentle demeanor. She was so tiny that her hands and feet
were hardly larger than my own. Barely taller than I
was, she had a round, pretty, open face and a childishly
musical voice that laughed gently with amusement
when she corrected us. I see now that she must have
been all of eighteen or nineteen, but to me at ten and
eleven she was the embodiment of the professional
dancer: I quickly adored her. She wore her dark hair
slicked back into the traditional dancer's bun with
artificial flowers woven around it, a look that I
instantly copied. Astrid could do anything, I thought,
watching her demonstrate for us the elementary steps
or mark a combination to perform in the center where
we felt that we were really dancing. Like Sonya, she
was apparently not quite authoritative enough to be
called by anything but her first name, but I still
thought Astrid the most beautiful woman I had ever
seen, the nicest, and by far the best dancer. Every
move she made looked effortless and graceful.

Because she was a teacher, Astrid had her own
dressing room, off to the side of the large one we all

shared, separated from us by a heavy curtain. The room was her domain, a privilege she enjoyed as our teacher, although she was hardly any older than I, just old enough for me to admire and emulate, as much as I could. Little by little she began to invite me into her room between classes, where we would sit side by side on a wooden bench facing a large mirror ringed with lights, the kind of mirror found in stage dressing rooms for stars. I silently watched her in the mirror while she swept up her long hair into a bun or lightly applied makeup to her eyes and mouth, observing her every movement so that I might try it later myself. As closely as I could, I imitated not only the style of her hair but the ease of her ballet style, her fluidity, her gestures, even (as I see now) her limitations and mistakes. From two classes a week, I moved to three, then four, and soon I was taking class daily, moving like an automaton from home to school to class and then home again, as ordinary life receded and the life of the ballet school took over. It happened so quickly and so inevitably that I never even thought about it, nor did I ever experience making a choice. I simply gave up the ordinary life of childhood for a different sort of freedom, the freedom of the barre and daily class.

When I got home from ballet school one day, I found four cotton dresses laid out on my single bed with its blue-and-white floral quilt. Three of the dresses were plaid—a Black Watch, a tan and brown tartan, a gray-and-yellow pattern—and one was a severe navy blue. All had long sleeves and prim, turned-down collars; all were fitted at the waist and all would reach an inch or two below my knees.

"You can pick out two," my mother said—or I could have three, or one, or whatever she thought I needed—as she did each time she repeated this ritual, buying clothes for me and then returning what I didn't want to the store. "Now that you're so involved at ballet school, there's no time for you to come shopping with me." So she brought home school dresses and soft lambswool cardigans that buttoned up the front with mother-of-pearl buttons, half slips and petticoats in white cotton, sometimes even winter coats, leaving them out in multiples on my bed for me to make the final choice.

That day I tried on each dress in front of the full-length mirror in my bedroom, my mother watching, and without much thought decided to keep the Black Watch plaid and the solid navy with the white collar. When I chose practice clothes I was a perfectionist, needing my leotards and tights and especially my soft leather ballet shoes to fit exactly, but with my everyday clothes I was just a little girl whose mother could dress her as she pleased in cotton or corduroy dresses each almost identical to the next, long-sleeved and cuffed in the winter and sleeveless in the summer, always with full skirts, fitted bodices decorated with rick-rack or smocking, and waists gathered in with sashes or cinch belts. She saw to it that beneath my dresses I always wore a slip, and when I needed a party dress, she sewed one for me, having brought home patterns for me to choose from and swatches of cloth. I chose a shimmering turquoise satin that my mother was luke-warm about but that I loved, and she let me have it anyway. In winter I might find on my bed a navy blue wool coat that weighed too heavily on my shoulders ("You'll grow into it"), and in spring a pink tweed coat flecked with red. Except for that one coat and what my mother sewed for special occasions, she always dressed me in dark colors—navy, dark green, different shades of brown. She cut my bangs, too, straight across my forehead like a little girl's, until I persuaded her that dancers always have long hair severely pulled back and began to let my bangs grow out. I wanted to look like Astrid.

Sometimes after class Astrid and I would have long intimate talks about *life*, like big and little sisters, rarely looking straight at each other but locking glances in the mirror, as if what Astrid might tell me was too uncomfortably truthful for a face-to-face talk. When she was most intimate, most open, she would glance away from the mirror as if to avoid her own reflection; I would follow her with my eyes until she returned to the mirror, ready for more conversation. In this way she confided in me that her parents had forbidden her to have a ballet career and that she hated them—*hated* them!—for forcing her to stay in school. She would leave home, she told me, her eyes flashing and her usually demure voice becoming almost harsh; she would run away to New York and "make it," she said grimly, and was instantly overcome with crying, her head in her hands and her small body heaving while I anxiously watched her in the mirror, not knowing how to comfort her. Trying to help and to offer the right words of consolation (How *could* they?! Yes, go to New York!), I felt large-boned and awkward, as if I were suddenly the teacher and this doll-like woman the pupil.

She did it, too; she ran away. One day she simply wasn't around, not in the studio teaching her Beginners Class nor in her little dressing room where we had our talks; and she couldn't be found the next day or the day after that. No one said a word about her or even seemed to notice she was gone, but I knew exactly where she was—in New York City auditioning for a ballet company. Making it. A month later she was back.

I waited for her outside her dressing room until she was finished teaching. "You ran away," I said breathlessly, wanting to hear every detail. Did F. know? What did her parents do? She admitted everything with a helpless shrug. Even F. had forbidden her to go, she confessed, and her parents had hired police and detectives who traced her to a women's hotel on East Fifty-seventh Street, where many dancers stayed. The police had returned her to her parents, who now kept her not quite under lock and key but at least under surveillance in case she should try again to bolt. Astrid's daring mesmermized me: To run away from home because your parents stood in your way, to elude detectives and police who would forcibly detain you, to give up everything for a ballet career seemed to me the pinnacle of devotion. My own parents, although noticeably busy with work and my younger brother and sisters, were too benign to run away from, and, besides, they quite likely lacked the theatrical panache to send out the militia to find me. I longed for wicked, evil parents whose mistreatment would compel me to run away for the sake of a great destiny.

But in any case, Astrid admitted, despite audition- ing for several ballet companies, she had not been able to find a job: Even the Rockettes at Radio City wouldn't take her; she was too short. Nothing she had hoped for had worked out. Her savings were depleted, so she hadn't argued with the detectives who had tracked her down but had accompanied them to an office where they telephoned her father. Once back with her parents, she had also returned to F., whom she had always worshiped. Luckily, he had forgiven her for running off and had taken her back, enfolding her again into the life of the studio. Nevertheless Astrid was visibly chastened; she looked as if she'd been repeatedly beaten. Did the police do anything to you?, I asked, imagining what I hoped was Astrid's heroic struggle against a phalanx of uniformed men, but she shook her head. A detective bought her a ticket and put her on a train, she said; he even gave her money for a sandwich. She could have run away again, but what was the point?

Astrid's life would now revolve entirely around F. He was her only hope, she confided, and she adored him more than ever. In addition to taking her own classes with him daily she was again teaching for him and would do whatever he wished. But from then on she looked perpetually bruised, even when she was cheerful, and she might fall silent for a few moments in the midst of one of our conversations. Sometimes she would cry quietly, still watching herself wide-eyed in the mirror, the tears glistening on her cheeks. At those times her face was pale; she seemed whitened, as if all her vitality had been blotted out.

Once or twice sitting next to Astrid on the bench, watching her in the mirror as she fixed her hair, I realized that F. had struck her with his cane: I could see the mark across her upper arm. "It's nothing," Astrid would say lightly, tightening the hairpins in her dancer's bun and fiddling with her earrings; F. had just corrected her in class, that's all. I met her eyes in the mirror while she reassured me; they glittered with pleasure almost as brightly as the diamond studs in her tiny earlobes. Clearly she had just come from what all dancers most enjoy: a good class.

So I knew from Astrid that F. was demanding and strict, quixotic and unpredictable, that he could hurt her and she wouldn't rebel. "Don't look so shocked," Astrid said, laughing at me. "How do you think you get to be a dancer?" I saw how exalted she felt at his attention, how the memory of being singled out by him made her turn her head away for a second and blush with a secret, intense pleasure.

Intermediate Class was more grueling than I had expected. In my second year in Intermediate II, I lost Astrid, for one thing, who stayed "behind" to teach Beginners, and instead I again had Sonya as my teacher, but now more demanding than Astrid and not at all the sunny, encouraging woman she had been during my first summer's lessons. Now Sonya was brassy and tough in class, with a harsh laugh and no hesitation about bantering with us or abrasively insulting us when we made mistakes. We were not children any longer, it seemed, to be indulged and encouraged with kind words; we were beginning to be dancers.

As it turned out, Intermediate Class also had a goal.

I had not foreseen that it would happen so soon, nor did I especially want it, but there it was before me: pointe shoes. We were "going on toe." Sitting in a semicircle at the end of class one day, we strapped on our new blocked shoes, tied the pink ribbons around our ankles, stood up and hobbled to the barre. The shoes were surprisingly weighty. I could barely walk in mine; my few steps to the barre to stand in first position were altogether ungainly. Clumsy. Also painful. Pointe shoes only *look* delicate; a new pair is actually brick solid. The sole is a thin sliver of stiff leather, malleable after being warmed and worked with for a while but at first like a piece of plywood. The blocked area around the toes is made only of hardened glue and satin, but hardened to a glaze that feels like wood. I felt as if a vise had tightened around my foot.

I learned later how to break in these shoes: You soften and bend them with warmth and pressure from your hands, working them over and over until they are pliable enough to put on, and then—tight as they are, and still completely unresilient—you may dip your whole foot, shoe and all, in a sinkful of water and walk around wet shod while the water softens the glue and the shoe dries molded to your foot. A quicker method is simply to pick up one shoe and bash it as hard as you can against a wall. A wooden floor does nicely, too, and a cement one is even better. *Thwack!* you will hear backstage or at ballet rehearsals.

Thud! Crack! "Oh, I'm just breaking in a new pair of shoes."

A professional dancer will spend less time actually dancing in her shoes than in sewing elastics and ribbons to them, darning the satin tips with a careful grid of heavy thread, and tirelessly breaking them in to the halcyon state of being soft enough to wear without embarrassing thuds against the stage. Only the strongest dancer can perform well with shoes that have become unblocked or whose arch can be bent in two.

The irony is that once the shoe is broken in, it will last for perhaps one performance, sometimes for only one ballet, until it is shredded from use. As is typical of ballet, there is that acme of perfection, even for shoes: one shining moment of perfectly broken-in pointe shoes, followed instantly by the precipitous drop back into imperfection and error. After that moment the quickly decrepit toe shoes are good only for practicing in class, *easy* class, or those early, experimental rehearsals when performance is still far away. For dancing full out, as dancers say, a dancer needs a new pair, perfectly broken in, Platonically ideal. Fragrant with new resin, fresh sweat.

But at my first session on pointe I was only barely aware of toe-shoe lore, although an older girl had been kind enough to show me at which exact spot inside the shoe to sew the double-faced pink ribbons. She also—from her lofty experience, or to bequeath me the masochistic impulse of dancers—told me that *professional* dancers don't use anything around their toes to protect them from the rubbing and chafing of the hardened glue. So I innocently slipped on my shoes—tugged them on, actually—with no cushioning. The other girls were smarter than I, or less ambitious, and had purchased little close-fitting caps of fur-lined moleskin to put over their neophyte toes, but I was determined to do it the right way, the professional way, and used nothing.

Facing the barre, with both hands holding on to it for placement and balance—for dear life, to be honest—we tried our first *relevé*. Usually you "roll up" to *relevé*, but my shoes were so stiff that I had to go from standing flat on the floor to full pointe with no plasticity, as if I were upending a board. But by the time we did the tiny, picky steps called *bourrées*, traveling down the barre to the right in a line and then back up again to the left, I had almost got the hang of it. I was clumsy but perfectly happy to totter up and down the barre doing *bourrées*. These *bourrées*, at first so painful and awkward to us, I learned later were the signature step for the Queen of the Wilis in the second act of *Giselle*: The malevolent queen flies from one end of the stage to the other in skimming *bourrées* so swift they can barely be seen. That, of course, is the focus of all ballet training: What begins in awkwardness and pain becomes through endless repetition and increasing artistry what is seen on stage—the human body in all its breathtaking loveliness.

In the beginning, though, I had to concentrate on not grabbing the barre with all my might, on not letting any of the disabling awkwardness show through as visible tension. No matter the effort, no evidence of pain or discomfort is allowed to show through the dancer's upper body or, most especially, on the face. But even if we didn't yet know about the Queen of the Wilis and her dazzling *bourrées*, we were on pointe at last, the pianist dutifully played real music for us, and we understood that we were part of the chain of artistry every dancer partakes of. Every Queen of the Wilis began, like us, at the barre.

We practiced on pointe that first day for all of fifteen minutes at the barre, never once letting go of it. When class was over and I sat down on the floor to remove my new shoes I found that the hard block encasing my toes had rubbed the skin: There were little bloody discs on my tights, one for each toe. I was proud of the blood, the evidence of my virgin effort, nor had I felt a second of pain once I had started to dance, my concentration had been so intense. But the next day our fifteen minutes on toe at the barre were agony; it was all I could do not to give up. And the day after that I succumbed and wrapped lambswool around my toes as I slipped on my shoes, but by this time the inner vamp of my shoe was brown with dried blood. For years I kept this first pair of shoes—bloodstained, tattered, and soft enough to fold in half—at the bottom of my closet as a souvenir. Every now and again I would take them out and look at them, always a little taken aback at how salted with sweat they seemed, how browned they were with dried blood, how reckless I had been not to shield myself more protectively when I had first used them.

Dancers jokingly call toe shoes "torture boots," but the pain and discomfort of these shoes, while not transitory, was overridden by my knowledge that they would, almost literally, transport me to a higher, more ethereal world. With pointe shoes I could in my imagination resemble some combination of my beloved Astrid and the legendary ballerina Marie Taglioni as she was portrayed in nineteenth-century lithographs. Taglioni was the first woman ever to go on pointe—a sylphide barely touching the ground in arabesque, a beatific expression on her face, her hair arranged in ringlets and crowned with a garland of flowers. Clearly the new invention of blocked shoes was for her a heavenly pleasure. So I quickly learned to apply moleskin to my feet when they weren't calloused enough to withstand the chafing and to use wisps of lambswool for padding. I would never be as benignly airborne or as ethereal as Taglioni, but if you had told me when I was twelve that ballet tradition mandated ringlets or splits in the air, I would have done my best to reproduce them.

With pointe shoes I began to learn how deeply a dancer relies on magical thinking to keep the universe under perfect balletic control. Every part of the shoe is sacred: Ribbons are sewed into the shoe at only one spot, the ends are knotted only under the anklebone and spit upon precisely lest they unravel. Many dancers in addition to their real pointe shoes wear a miniature set of crossed shoes on a necklace, as if wearing a talisman or a religious medal.

As tradition dictated, I spent hours darning the pink satin block of every pair of new shoes, always put my left shoe on first, always crossed the inside ribbon over the outside ribbon, always applied spit to the knot. Later I would go on to learn other inviolate customs of the ballet world, the ones that lend a mystical aura to performing: A dancer, for example, always says *merde* to mean "good luck" to someone about to perform (to say "good luck" is considered bad luck), and without fail prays and crosses herself frantically in the wings, sometimes over and over, before flinging herself onstage. These codes are so deeply engrained in my body's memory that even today I always put on my left shoe first, even though it is no longer a pointe shoe but perhaps a sneaker or a boot. If somehow I forget or deliberately deviate from the habit, I am uneasy until I start over again and correct the mistake.

At the end of my first year on toe, while I was still an Intermediate dancer in Sonya's class, the ballet school mounted a performance of *Sleeping Beauty*. I thought of what we did as a performance, but in the careful hierarchies of ballet lingo it was called a "demonstration," to signal that we were still only students. The event was certainly not a recital, we were carefully told; a recital was beneath us, something put on by what our teachers scathingly referred to as "other ballet schools." *We* were not just any school; we were the F. Ballet Academy, named after F. himself, with its high standards and roster of venerable teachers. But our *Sleeping Beauty* seemed authentic to me: Even though it was only a two-act production, we had lavish costumes, an orchestra, and professional dancers in the lead roles. Only later did I realize how much the choreography had been watered down to a level that even we Intermediate students could perform. I, who in truth could still barely dance at all, who was still awkwardly close to being a Beginner, was part of a large crowd of students dancing the ballet's famous waltz. Although I recall little about the entire production, I can still remember—my body remembers—the exact choreography of our waltz in Act 1 to the lilting Tchaikovsky music and the costume I wore, with its pink satin bodice and long, gauzy, rainbow-colored skirt.

But what I remember most vividly was standing in the wings during the performance itself and looking out onto the stage, where, in the center of a cone of light, I saw a little girl named Carlotta Carrera doing an absolutely perfect *attitude en pointe*. I hardly knew Carlotta, but at that moment on stage she seemed more luminously birdlike than human, a tiny, raven-haired, dark-skinned creature dressed in a bright yellow tutu that looked almost oversize for such a small body. She was so fragile that even her toe shoes seemed bulkier than her legs. Standing in the wings, looking out onto the wide, cavernous stage, darkened except for that one cone of light, I was overcome by Carlotta: the enchantment of bright yellow against her dark skin and the spotlit, lovely perfection of her pose.

Because of Carlotta Carrera's perfectly poised *attitude en pointe* in her vibrant yellow tutu, I fell in love with dancers' names. All the most talented ones seemed to have names as exquisite as they themselves were, names as beautiful as Carlotta Carrera, names that evoked a world of alliterative, rhythmic harmonies. Maria Callisto, with her mass of curly red hair, brown eyes, and exquisitely arched feet. Little Natalya Tolstoi, who spoke Russian and whose sad-eyed mother seemed to be a friend of F.'s. Rosemary

O'Meara. Fiona Drayton. My Beginners teacher, Astrid Aalgard. Tenley Manning. Elizabeth Edwards. Clea Cassidy. Olivia Eckstein. Dana Freed. Alexandra Mirofsky. Even the name of my best friend, Martine Recanati. But my own name was so unimaginative and discordant, so unfeminine, that I was in despair over it. If one's name were one's fate, with a pedestrian name like mine, I would never become a dancer. Even F. realized the problem of my name and would occasionally rename me, Russian-style: "E-von-itsch," he would say affectionately, but as if I were a boy, or, better, "Vanoushka." *Before I become a great dancer,* I thought, *I will have to change my name.*

After *Sleeping Beauty* the Royal Ballet came to town, and I was chosen, along with many other children, as a "super," an extra, to fill out the crowd scenes in the Royal's *Petrouchka*. At our one rehearsal where all our movements were carefully explained and the patterns were blocked, I found out that my job was to roam the stage under the supervision of my "mother," a Royal Ballet corps de ballet dancer, and then to ride on a carousel at stage right along with my "sister." On the day of the first performance, I unfortunately came down with a bad case of flu, but my real mother, to my immense gratitude, filled me with aspirin, put me in the back seat of our car along with a pillow and a pile of blankets, and drove me, feverish and shivering, to the theater. Backstage in the dressing room I told no one I was sick and conquered my dizziness long enough to get into costume and makeup and out onto the stage, where I was instantly staggered by the heat of the lights, their intense brightness, and the cast of professional dancers whirling around me.

I had fleeting moments of guilt for infecting the entire Royal Ballet with my flu, but the joy of performing on the same stage with them overrode all my compunctions. Dazzled—and dizzy with fever—I could watch to my heart's content the famous dancers whom before I had only heard of and read about; I could listen in on their chatter and see them nervously warming up backstage. I watched them paw the resin box with their ballet slippers or toe shoes seconds before they catapulted themselves on stage into their own performances, felt the spray of sweat coming from them as they whirled and jumped around me, saw them double over in the wings, heaving and panting for air, when they finished their solo variations.

The stage was so crowded, and I was so dizzily overcome with heat and motion and fever that I completely (and luckily) missed my carousel ride—I never even saw the carousel until too late—and was shepherded offstage, where I promptly fainted in the dressing room. "Excitement," the woman in charge of costumes said matter-of-factly, ignoring me in the crush of adults and children rushing in from the stage and rushing out to perform again. I was still hotly exhilarated when my mother came to fetch me, pumping me full of more aspirin and bundling me up again in her blankets. The next day I was so sick that I couldn't get out of bed. My understudy had to go onstage that night and ride the carousel in my stead, but I didn't care—I had danced *Petrouchka* with the Royal! A few days later I was back in class, strapping on my pointe shoes and trying to master my *relevés* and *piqué* turns.

F., when I was "invited" into his class, was gaunt and beaky and silent. He barely ever spoke to us in Russian, much less in English, although later I would acquire from him an extensive vocabulary of Russian threats, insults, and curse words, all of them spoken to me with the utmost courtesy and wry reserve. When he spoke English, it was almost always to insult. "You look like a dog peeing at a hydrant," he would say churlishly, or, "You're flopping around like a fish," or, "Your hands are flowerpots." But mostly, instead of speaking, F. whistled with a volume that would stop traffic and that sounded to me like an entire orchestra.

He whistled constantly—even now the sounds of his whistling echo in my memory, each note sheering off into new harmonies and chains of sound, each melody amplified so that he seemed to be whistling whole chords at once. Sardonic and moody in his infrequent speech, he sketched movements and combinations with fleeting gestures of his hands, a cigarette askew in his mouth, but when he walked through the class during barre exercises he whistled exuberantly, accompanying every movement with a different tune. To indicate to the pianist what tempo he wanted, or what tune, he whistled. He whistled to start class, to call us in, to dismiss us. Did he whistle because he spoke and thought more easily in Russian; was his English inadequate? I don't remember ever thinking that he spoke in a "foreign" way or with an accent, but perhaps I was so quickly used to the polyglot language of ballet—French, Russian, English, a smattering of other languages, not to mention all those whistles, taps, and hand signals—that any sounds used in any fashion made ballet sense.

When he wasn't whistling, he might be cursing us in Russian, which had its own melody. But dancers themselves learn silence and often say nothing at all, certainly nothing in class unless they are daring—or foolhardy. Dancers learn that they are bodies only, speaking through their bodies, expressive with their bodies rather than with words; they use language mostly to acknowledge how far they are from perfection, the Platonic ideal of form. Mostly, dancers are allowed only to nod and to say "Yes, sir" or "Yes, madame." Otherwise the only other word they are given to say is "sorry." The litany is said repeatedly, under one's breath: "Sorry . . . Sorry . . . Sorry, my fault."

To indicate satisfaction or, more accurately, to indicate *approaching* satisfaction—satisfaction that might be reached if only one's body were not so defiantly unmanageable, if only one could concentrate better, work harder—but nonetheless to indicate the dangerously ephemeral pleasure of having done something well, even if not perfectly, a dancer will say, "It's coming." There is a great hazard to that allowance; more often than not, whatever is "coming" will immediately disappear and one will be back to nodding mutely or apologizing, stoical but defeated.

Along with his whistles F. gestured intricately with his hands to let us know what combination of steps we were supposed to dance. Usually he would single me out from the group, place me in the center of the ballet studio, and with tiny, minute tremblings of his fingers and wrists "tell" me what we were to dance next. I would then demonstrate for the class, which afterward would replicate what I had performed. Sometimes he would give me a verbal cue: *"Chassé, saut de basque, piqué, piqué,"* he might say, using his hands for the rest of the combination. "Yes?" he would ask, making sure that I understood his shorthand. I would nod and do it.

Of course he also carried a thin, pliable leather cane with which he would rhythmically beat out time against the barre or the floor, keeping the beat of the piano music even when he was whistling something completely different. Sometimes he used his cane as if it were musical notation, pointing with it, balancing it on a finger, twirling it or spinning it around to indicate pirouettes. With his cane he also corrected us with a tap on the shoulder or wrist or thigh, and hit us when our bodies were obdurate or when the mood struck him. He would hit quickly and hard, out of the blue, like an exclamation point, *So!* Only his favorite students were struck, the chosen ones. The others were ignored no matter what they did.

When I would describe to Astrid some harsh insult F. had lacerated me with in class that day or mention casually that, yes, he had struck my wrist because it was "broken" in arabesque, Astrid would listen carefully. The harsher he was to me the more it pleased Astrid, as if F.'s insults confirmed my promise as a dancer and how well she had trained me. Then, sitting on her bench and looking into her mirror, we would both together practice our "arabesque arms," Astrid's, of course, perfectly modeled and placed. I learned that if F. struck my wrist because it "broke," it never did that again nor should I ever object. The wrist "remembered," it straightened out, and my *line*—that ineffable, Platonic line—was a fraction closer to the ideal.

In my first days in Advanced, I also learned the name of the girl who would stand next to me every day at the barre—the wild and joyful Martine, who quickly became my best friend. Ballet students eye each other carefully, assessing each newcomer's strengths and weaknesses and tacitly assigning rank in class, from "best" to "not worth paying attention to." When I arrived, Martine was F.'s clear favorite, all strength and sharp edges, with an athletic, forceful style: Unlike me, she would throw herself into anything, risk the big jumps and multiple turns whether she could accomplish them or not. In looks, too, she was my opposite: A year or two older than I, she was dark, skinny, and wiry, with high cheekbones and dark eyes that slanted upward as if she were Tatar or Mongolian. To amuse me, she would slant her eyes even further with her fingertips, announcing with a broad accent, "I Rrrooossian peasant. Here to be grrreat prrrima ballerrrina," and would dip to the floor in a deep curtsy, histrionically blowing kisses off her fingertips to her supposedly wildly applauding audience. Although she adored and feared F. as much as any of us, Martine would slyly make fun of him behind his back, mocking his blithe carriage as he made his walks around the studio or the way he sat coiled up in a chair when we did center work, watching us dourly. When he was insulting, she would sidle up to me at the barre to whisper commentaries in my ear, making sure that F. didn't catch her and throw her out of class. "All talk," she would say dismissively, although we both knew that wasn't quite true. "What a show." Or she would look stern and raise her hand, saying in her best Russian accent, "I hit you, no? *Then* you rrrememberrr."

F., although I and all my classmates revered him, was himself only a lesser figure in a legendary ballet dynasty. Russian, of course. I knew from the ballet history books that everyone in his family for generations had been dancers, teachers, great choreographers, and that his mother had been in her day a reigning prima ballerina. Occasionally she would visit the studio and our Advanced Class as if she were an emissary from the Old World or a star from a distant galaxy. On those rare visits she would "take" us, teach our class herself, while F. stood unobtrusively at her side, uncharacteristically subdued and deferential. In her eighties, she still bobbed about on her little bird legs, done up Russian-style in fishnet tights, chirping to us young girls in Russian, the only language she knew. "You speak Russian?" she would chirp at me, in English-Russian. "No, Madame," I would answer, ballet-style, in English-French. She would then shriek at me in Russian—abuse, I supposed, or astonishment that these young American girls who wanted to be great dancers couldn't even speak Russian—all the while darting about on pointe in her ballet slippers.

"Feet of steel," we would say to each other afterward. It was a great day when Madame F. came to class; we felt as if History had just blown through the door of the studio in fishnet tights and soft, unblocked ballet shoes. Through her we could see the whole ballet tradition, from Petipa through Cechetti down to us in our late childhood standing at the barre and practicing our *pliés*. Despite its French and Italian influences, it was basically a Russian tradition we inherited, a grand and hyperbolic one of Russian "soul," extreme demands on the body for high elevations and extensions and bravura feats of technique. Somehow in F.'s class we always heard the distant roll of applause, just as in Martine's mockery. In our imaginations we received extravagant bouquets of red roses, looked on with gracious surprise as suitors and excited fans drank champagne from our immaculate pointe shoes.

In one of my early days in F.'s class, we were all practicing arabesques, first arabesque, second arabesque, third arabesque, in turns or *promenade*. Now we were doing combinations of arabesques in the center, ending in a long *arabesque penché*, in which, standing on one leg, you lean to the floor, tilting your arabesque until you come almost to a vertical split in the air. I loved doing these movements: I was naturally limber, my extensions were high, and I was moved by the slow, sweet, lyrical quality of the music where one could fill out the melodies, embody them, rather than jump on top of the notes as one often had to in the quicker, more bravura parts of the class.

F. was watching me closely without saying a word. When we finished the combination and paused before beginning again, he walked over and stood behind me.

"Arabesque," he demanded.

I stretched out one arm and one leg in arabesque. From behind, he placed one hand on my chest, right under my breasts, and his other under my out-stretched leg. Then pressing on me with both hands, he folded me upward until my raised leg and my upper body, both stretched upward toward the ceiling, formed a V. It felt wonderful, as if my body were made of thin, pliable wire meant to be molded into this new shape.

"Look in the mirror," he told me. He sounded gentle, private.

I glanced at myself. I had never before seen an arabesque like mine before—so high, so sharply etched. I looked away.

"No, no, look at yourself," he urged me, taking his hands away from me for a few seconds like a sculptor dazzled by his own creation while I held my high arabesque without his help. "See what you can do? Do you see how beautiful you are?"

Yes, I saw. F. had given me my own beauty with his touch—not only with the quick, violent slash of his cane or the gentle insistence of his hands, but with some radiant promise that I would become as beautiful as he saw me.

I felt claimed by F.'s touch on my body, however it was meted out. No matter how full of watchfulness I was around him, how exalted or apprehensive I might be rendered by his attention or his threats, I allowed F. to do as he wished. I trusted him; and not only did I trust his vision for me, but I trusted him with my body. Entirely.

So even though I had lost my breath in amazement and shock when F. first struck me, it had never occurred to me to gather up my dance case from under the barre and run out of the studio and home. Nor had I felt any consternation from the other girls in the class; we had all simply continued *battements tendus* as if nothing had happened. Certainly no one intervened on my behalf. If precise and direct punishment meted out with a cane made one a great dancer, then I welcomed the pain, the submission, the promise it held out. When F. touched me in arabesque, folded me upward into a perfect V, I could see with my own eyes that the pain was worth it.

For dancers, for whom speech is pared down as much as their bodies, and who live hours a day in their classes without speaking at all, touch is a special language. Ballet touching is full of signs, meanings understood by dancers each in its own context. Anyone can touch you, anywhere. But the way you are touched, and when, and by whom, is a code; every dancer knows it and is always alert to it. When your best girlfriend, someone like Martine, say, grabs your ankle when you are practicing your extensions, stretching in the air, and pushes your leg up as high as it will go in *développé à la seconde*, and then higher, higher, until your legs practically make a split in the air, she is still just your friend, helping you out. Maybe fooling around. You might grimace with pain or moan something like, "Oh my God, that's enough!" or even, "Keep going, it feels great!" Then, of course, you return the favor. "Now I'll do you," you say, holding out your hand for her to rest her foot in so that you can start tugging it upward. Or you and Martine might lie together on the floor, each of you touching yourself all over, pulling your legs out for stretches, rubbing the sore places. "Do you think this muscle is too tight?" she might ask, and you press your fingers there, deep into her skin, to test it out and·then help her pound it with the sides of your hand, akin to the way one tenderizes meat. Dancers touch each other like this all the time; they examine each other's bodies and their own in every hard and soft place.

But when your ballet teacher stretches your body, checks your placement, assesses your body's resistance, watches your face, you don't say a word; you keep yourself impassive, benign. You surrender to him—I surrendered to F.—to his will, to his hope for what pattern my body should make in space, how it should move and look. Then I was not fooling around: It was something serious. Then his touch felt like love.

But often enough F.'s touch was neither brutal nor tender; rather it was practical, businesslike. Just a finger across my brow. He would position himself near me as I practiced at the barre but barely pay any attention to me at all, looking for all the world as if he had nothing more to do than lean on the barre, a cigarette in his hand, as relaxed and dapper as any guy leaning against a lamppost as a girl saunters by. As I struggled and worked through my exercises, he might suddenly turn to me and draw a finger across my forehead, then hold it straight down, counting the beads of sweat as they formed at his fingertip and slowly fell to the floor. "If I can't get three drops," he would say, "you're not working hard enough."

After class, I was slick, dripping, my face sometimes so far beyond flushed that it would be greenish white. My first stop was the water fountain, at which there was always a line. There I streamed water into my mouth and spit it out, since dancers are taught not to gulp water when they are overheated but to wait until their bodies gradually return to a normal temperature. I would hold my wrists under the spray to cool down my blood (so I thought) and splash cupped water on my face. In the dressing room I would peel off my practice clothes, towel myself dry, wad up my leotard and tights into a damp ball and pack them back into my hatbox with my towel and shoes. Two things were absolutely necessary in this ritual: the hatbox, the then-fashionable carrying case that identified dancers, and a bottle of Jean Naté Friction Pour le Bain, which we all liberally splashed on ourselves before and after class. Everything smelled of Jean Naté, and everything was damp. Even my ballet shoes were soggy. My pointe shoes, whose satin sides I would carefully fold inward after class, molding the thin wooden shank into a curve and wrapping the ribbons carefully around the stem of the shoe, tucking in the ends—my pointe shoes were limp, fragrant with musty wood and the honeyed dampness of glue.

When I left the studio I always headed for the drugstore. I was parched. The drugstore was my oasis, where every day I sat—still flushed—at the counter and ordered, invariably, a glass of tomato juice with lemon, please. Not ready to go home just yet, warm and exhilarated from my class with F., I wanted to linger over refreshment, the sweetness of tomato juice cut by the fresh-squeezed lemon. It was served with ice and a straw in a tall curved glass, the kind of glass from which girls drank Coke in movies, sipping through their straws and swinging their legs while waiting for a boyfriend to amble by. I sat on a revolving stool, spinning slightly so that my skirt fanned out around my legs, and sipped my tomato juice, my hatbox beside me, everything fragrant with the distinctive note of Jean Naté. I imagined myself a girl in a musical—that carefree girl swiveling around on a stool, sipping my drink, ready for the next adventure.

Once I had left dance and F. was no longer part of my life, I never ordered another glass of tomato juice, ever, although now if one were placed in front of me, with ice cubes and a wedge of lemon, it would loosen a particle of memory: I would become thirteen again, light bodied and stretched out, still lightly perspiring, just out of class.

But sometimes when my body "remembers," I hear no words, no counts out loud to define the music, no verbal signals. Just a rapping on the floor with the ballet master's cane, and the wordless comprehension that an entire roomful of dancers will turn in unison toward the barre or step into fifth position in the center to begin the exercise again. The music will start and dancers will move through it automatically, responding to kinetic memory, doing the same combination of steps over and over, trying to get them right. Dancers always try harder, and then try harder again. "Begin again," the ballet master says, and even though we are dripping with sweat, we are gulping air, our chests are heaving, we take our places in the center of the studio and start the exercise, the choreography, all over again. Perfectly poised, oxygen coursing madly through us, every muscle of our bodies exhilarated and ready for the challenge, we take our places and without a word begin again.

Even now, now that I am no longer a dancer but a wholly ordinary real person, if I hear the music to, say, *Les Sylphides* or *Swan Lake*, ballets I have danced in rehearsal and in performance countless times, my body listens and obeys. I can be unmoving, stationary, seated in a crowded audience, but with the familiar music my body in its immobility and inwardness performs the accustomed choreography: I am perfectly still but every cell of my body dances.

F. had what I always thought of as a secret room. It was on a landing all to itself, reached by walking down a long empty corridor and then knocking on a heavy door. Officially F.'s secret room was his office, although clearly not a shred of work could possibly get done there. For real work F. had a very public desk in the "teacher's area" of the lobby opposite the ballet classrooms, where he would sometimes sit and pore over papers, oblivious to the dancers stretching and erupting into little warm-up jumps around him. While he worked, Sonya might sit on the desk, her legs crossed and her back to F., smoking and taking attendance. Even Astrid sometimes sat behind F.'s desk when he wasn't around, looking especially miniature and wide-eyed, as if she were playing at being a grown-up.

But the secret room was another story. "What

could he be doing in there?" we would ask one another, always aware that when F. wasn't visible in the lobby or the classrooms, he had enclosed himself in his private space, not to be disturbed. Getting away from Sonya, we would speculate. Cheering up Astrid so she wouldn't try to run away again to New York to join the Rockettes. "Just taking a nap," Martine would announce with supercilious hauteur, as if she had checked.

I kept quiet. I certainly didn't want anyone to know that I had been there often, the door locked behind me and every item in that room fixed indelibly in my memory. The room itself was small and crowded, furnished with a couch, one or two chairs, a small wooden table, a refrigerator, and, most importantly, an elaborately carved mahogany sideboard that turned out to house a shortwave radio, the only one I had ever seen. F. would summon me to his room with a wave of his hand and a nod in the direction of the hallway, or a note would be passed to me in the dressing room with a quizzical look that I ignored. "Go to my office," the note would say in barely legible handwriting. At that moment I felt as if I were headed for the guillotine. My journey down the long hallway felt like the victim's last walk, and while I didn't dare disobey the summons, I never went quickly or joyfully either. In fact, when I realized I would have to join F. in his secret room I did my best to turn off sensation entirely, to go on automatic, setting the dials for my destination without registering what might await me once I arrived.

What so set me on edge in F.'s summons to his room was that I simply could not predict what would happen once I was there, just the two of us locked in and no one else around. Sometimes, although rarely, I was curtly reprimanded or even punished for some misstep or assumed inattention in that day's class. At those times he would hit me—once—while I stood dutifully still as if it were just another ballet exercise at the barre or part of the choreography. *"Passé,"* he would say, pointing with his cane and tapping my right foot as it traveled up my left leg to *passé*, where I would freeze in what I hoped was perfect placement until he hit me sharply across my hip to remind me never, *never* to raise it. *Now* could I remember? Yes, I would nod. Then F. would smile at me with ironic complicity, courteously hold the door open for me, and I would leave, often without having spoken a word.

But just as likely it was not punishment that awaited me but companionship and even conversation. I would knock on the door, F. would greet me cordially, and then ceremoniously pour a glass of ginger ale for me and a tumbler of vodka for himself, after which I would curl up on the couch for an intimate chat. What I especially wanted F. to tell me were stories of his childhood, of his boyhood days at the ballet academy in St. Petersburg, where his family had been renowned for generations, his mother had been a prima ballerina, and his uncle had been a famous choreographer. That's where I longed to be: I could easily imagine myself crossing the snowy streets and canals of St. Petersburg to get to the Imperial Ballet School, whose classroom floors were raked at exactly the same angle as the Maryinsky stage on which they would perform, and the girls changed into their practice clothes beneath portraits of the czars. Despite how avidly I romanticized F.'s boyhood at the Maryinsky Theater—as if I were listening to Tamara Karsavina's *Theatre Street*, which my parents had given me as a birthday gift and which I passionately read over and over—F. would vouchsafe these snippets of autobiography reluctantly, almost bitterly, letting me know somehow, in the interstices of conversation, that his life in the ballet world had not gone quite as he had hoped. Rather than dwell on his childhood, however, he preferred to veer off into stories of his three marriages, his children, how bitterly disappointing they all were.

Often he complained to me about his first two wives, Sonya's predecessors. From an album, he handed me large, carefully preserved photographs of the two prior wives—both were Russian, he said, and certainly both were blonds and indistinguishably pretty. I couldn't imagine how F. could tell the wives apart: The photos showed them dressed alike in two-piece, halter-topped bathing suits, cavorting on a beach with children and beach balls, their long legs muscled like dancers', their hair pulled back under scarves. What had happened to those remote wives F. didn't let on, but he had fathered a child with at least one of them, a son who was now "very American," he told me disdainfully, a lawyer or a stockbroker. (Could I actually have heard the word *stockbroker* from F.? The word sticks in my memory as if from a different galaxy, light-years away from the Russian and French ballet-talk that always swirled around me, or F.'s reminiscing about his St. Petersburg boyhood. What was a *stockbroker* doing in that secret room?) In any case, the "American" son had taken a path different from his dancer father, and had even produced a blond, "American" granddaughter whom F. described with a mixture of pride and odd indifference. F. passed me a photograph of the little girl at the beach: She seemed much younger than I, robust and healthy, smiling into the camera in full sunlight. Not for her the warm, dusty light of a ballet studio, let in meagerly through windows tilted open just enough to block out any cooling breeze. Neither I nor F. seemed to know what to make of her. F. just looked wryly at the photograph, shrugged his shoulders in apparent disbelief, and a second later took it out of my hands.

But more than talking to me of his disappointing family, he liked to tell me of other dancers he had trained, all of whom to me were the most exotic and amazing of stars. If I were lucky that day and F. was in a good mood, he would compare me to what he had known of them as young ballet students. "You remind me of so-and-so," he would say, cheerfully, naming perhaps the one dancer I most admired and wished to emulate. Just as I was beginning to glow with pleasure, he would add, "No brain," and press two fingers onto his forehead as if he had a headache. "All air in there," he would say with a wicked gleam in his eyes or a wink. "Not strong. Muscles like bubble gum."

I never knew of F. attending a ballet performance (in fact, it never occurred to me to endow him with a life outside the studio and his secret room—that is, a life away from me). But he had opinions of everyone, canonical and final. The ineffable quality he looked for in dancers and admired more than technique was what he called "personality" or "emotion." If a dancer had "no personality," F. would dismiss her with a wave of his hand. That was it; she was beneath considera-tion. But when a dancer had "too much personality," even if F. said so sardonically with a shrug of his shoulders, he seemed to be awarding a great compli-ment. Russian dancers had "too much personality," clearly; it was F.'s accolade for them. It meant that the dancers were daring, burned up space, breathed fire. I would rather have had *too much personality* than not enough, whatever the risk.

Alicia Alonso, the Cuban prima ballerina, was his darling and definitely had too much personality. She had once been his pupil and returned to him for a private lesson when she was in town. When Alonso came to the studio, F. would invite me to watch her class: I would sit quietly in a corner of the studio and drink in her every move, from her beginning *demi-pliés* to the clear, perfect turns she did at the hour's end. Even though I was just an onlooker, an anonymous neophyte, for a rapturous hour the beauty of the universe was in that studio, the three of us linked there by our devotion to formal perfection and allegiance to ballet tradition. But what surprised me at first was how young Alonso looked, even though when I first saw her she must have already been an "aging" ballerina, a dancer perhaps even in her forties. Yet in her practice clothes and woolen leg warmers she was as lithe as a teenager, attractive and giggling. Everything about her was dynamic, from her jet black hair, wide eyes, and beautiful carriage to the dramatic way she performed even the simplest exercise at the barre. F. was tender to her, sometimes amused, and even brutal, the way he was with me, and he whistled as if he had a room full of girls and not just one solitary ballerina. He whistled and paced up and down the room, but always came back to Alonso to correct her, to reposition her gently but deftly and with intense focus. The energy he would normally expend on a class full of dancers went entirely to her.

Much later, with F.'s classes and his secret room hidden in my most private memory, I was on tour with a ballet company when we were joined by Alonso as our guest artist, by now much more ancient than she had been in F.'s class and frighteningly blind. She had to be led to the wings by an assistant and would squint and tap her way to the stage with her pointe shoes until she heard the cue to her music; then she would dance as if she owned the universe. One night during a performance of the pas de deux from *Don Quixote*, the music had already started for the ballerina's variation when Alonso suddenly halted in midstep. She put up her hand to stop the orchestra, walked with perfect aplomb to center stage with the spotlights blazing on her, and nodded to the conductor.

"Begin again, Maestro, please," she ordered. And Maestro did exactly as he was told, of course. From where I was watching in the wings, I knew that F. would have growled "too much emotion," but loved her for it—her daring, her impetuousness, her imperious conceit. Her rule breaking. He wanted dancers who broke rules, who were headstrong.

Several times in the secret room F. handed me a small, black-and-white snapshot, always in silence and with a look that suggested he was sharing contraband or initiating me into something forbidden. This picture showed a young man—F. himself, years before—partnering a Russian ballerina who, to my eyes, looked trustingly childlike. He was standing a few feet away from the woman, almost crouching, with only one outstretched hand holding her steady in arabesque, almost as if he couldn't deign to touch her. It was an insolent, feral gesture. F.'s partnering of this woman had a savage undertone that I was never to see on stage: Staring at the photograph made me feel like an interloper or a voyeur, uneasily drawn into this esoteric pas de deux. Adding to my discomfort, one body was clothed, the other assertively exposed. It was the woman who was softly curved and fully costumed for the stage in an old-fashioned gauze tutu, a turban wrapped around her hair, while F. was wearing what seemed to be only a jockstrap. Otherwise he was naked. You could see the long muscles of his thighs, deeply indented, and the crisscross of muscles across his taut abdomen. He looked lean, sinewy, underfed, like a stray dog or wolf.

I would hold the snapshot gingerly, knowing that F. was watching my face for a reaction. I never knew what to say, but couldn't take my eyes from the man's aggressively naked body and the deliberate way he secured the woman with one hand. Held on pointe in arabesque, she reminded me of Astrid's gift, the ballerina charm I wore around my neck, except that a man's hand was on her ribs. In silence I would give back the snapshot, relieved to be rid of it until the next time F. decided to confront me with images of women he had known.

Sometimes, instead of conversation and photographs, F. would open the mahogany cupboard and turn on his shortwave radio so that the two of us could listen to what seemed to be a news broadcast from Russia. We never listened to music; it was always the spoken voice, racing and garbled, overlaid by static, as if tanks and rifles could overwhelm it at any second. But whether or not I understood the language was entirely irrelevant to me; even when the language was English, the bond F. had inaugurated with me and in which I was complicit was outside language; it had to be wordless, *in*explicit, since by its very nature it demanded silence. I was in that office with F. for reasons I would never have articulated. What was said or not said, or whether in Russian, French, or English, was not the point; what I knew was that I had entered that room willingly rather than flee the building forever, and that once inside I was captive to whatever, out of his capriciousness, F. might bestow. More than captive: I would surrender to him immediately, to whatever he demanded. I also knew that I would never say a word to anyone.

Everything that occurred in that room I accepted without question as an immutable law of the universe.

If I sometimes bantered with F. there, or hungrily listened to his stories, it took enormous energy—and wariness—to seem sweetly relaxed, since my usual habit in that room was to erase myself, to be perfectly compliant until the door was opened again and I was released. Yet once I was released, I wanted nothing more than to return, to be summoned back.

When F. called me to his secret room, I went in alone and left alone; no one ever accompanied me. Not Martine, or Astrid, or any of the other girls in my ballet classes. Even though Martine was my best friend and constant companion, I never so much as hinted to her that I joined F. at the end of the long hallway, making sure that no one saw me enter or leave. For me, that room was a space unlike any I ever could have imagined, full of the dangerous and unspoken possibility that F. might in that private world once more look at me quizzically, asking, *Do you want it again?*

What if in his secret room I might say to F. what I could not possibly have said at the barre: *Yes, please. Yes, I do want it again. Please. Please* is one of the most erotic words in the language, capable of infinite nuance. Sometimes it is beseeching. It means that you are asking for it, begging for it, politely or abjectly, almost against your will. You are divided: You desire something whether you want it or not. Language doesn't have words for how divided I felt against myself; we have oxymorons, paradoxes, but no word that lets us know that we are there for the taking, that we will do anything, although the risk is so appalling as to be unthinkable. There, hidden at the end of a hallway in F.'s room, I was there for the taking: F. knew it and I knew it, too, although I could not have said so. The only word we have for such submission, such acquiescence, is "please." A silence, a breath taken in and released. *Yes, please.*

If outside that room F. was indisputably the ballet master whose every word I obeyed, inside that room our connection was more varied, nourished by food and drink, warmed by our talking together and buffeted by our strange silences. When I watched F. bustle about like a good host, getting the ice tray, pouring our drinks, fiddling with the dials of the radio, I thought he was the most dangerous and beautiful man I had ever seen. When he was displeased or irritable, my body felt tense and coiled, jarred by F.'s slightest move, but when he surprised me by hovering over me and taking care of me as if I were a special guest, I became almost languorous. No matter his mood, though, he was unfailingly courtly. He never sat down until I was seated, waving to me playfully to make myself at home on his couch and handing me my ginger ale with a mock bow. Sitting Indian fashion on his couch in my practice clothes and ballet slippers, I couldn't take my eyes from him, aware of his every gesture and shift of position. It pleased him, I could tell, to be the center of my world even while he liked waiting on me, serving me his treats and eager for me to savor them. Sometimes he poured schnapps for both of us in little shot glasses. Then he would raise his glass to me in a toast and we would both polish off our drinks Russian-style, in one gulp.

Once, while I was sipping my ginger ale in F.'s secret room, F. decided to add some cheese as an hors d'oeuvre. Without asking me whether or not I liked cheese or wanted it, he took a wedge from the refrigerator and began to slice it, lodging the thin slices in my mouth piece by piece, as if I were a baby bird. As he sliced, however, the knife slipped—he gashed his finger. Holding his hand up over the cheese, he let a drop of blood fall on the slice, then held the cheese to my mouth. "Eat," he ordered. Obediently I opened my mouth. F. put the bloody sliver on my tongue as if it were a communion wafer, and I swallowed it.

It fascinated me that he demanded of me arduous tasks, proofs of devotion, that I never had imagined before I entered Advanced Class, as if F. himself were leading me in stages to ever higher realms of balletic perfection. If wearing bloody toe shoes were a proof of one's self-discipline and devotion to artistry, then why not swallowing bloody cheese? "Do you want it again?" I always hear F. asking in the background, and

I can see myself nodding *Yes*, acquiescing to these rites of initiation and commitment. The real world—the world of parents and school and friendships—seemed farther and farther away each time I entered F.'s secret room, never knowing what dramas I would encounter there, what layers of love or violence, what invitations to obedience and silence. Sometimes nothing happened at all, but even that *nothing* held a universe of possibility.

When F. was disconsolate—or angry—he would brood silently at the far window for a long time, standing with his back to me while I stood in the doorway and watched him. Waited for him to turn around. With his back turned, he seemed to be threatening me, but what exactly the threat was or how it might be carried out I couldn't tell. I loved that sensation of fear, even though it sickened me a little. Nor was I so much frightened by his ominous silence as aroused and expectant, expecting something so mysterious that I had no language for it, something palpable but unnamed. When he turned around, finally, he would look me up and down broodingly as if he had never really seen me before, even though he was as familiar with my body as I was. I would stand still, letting him examine me while I deliberately held myself stationary as if I were posing, my arms crossed behind me like the Degas statue of the ballet girl. I thought, *I can never tell anyone how we just stand here looking at each other.*

Did I go to school once I entered Advanced Class? Did I have parents? teachers? Of course I did; I wasn't an orphan. But once F. had claimed me, it was as if the entire rest of the world dimmed. My real and intense life was at the ballet school with F.: Everything else receded into the far distance, almost as if it were happening to someone else. I wanted to dance, that was it. Nothing else mattered.

It is hard for me to remember, but surely outside the ballet school I became just another thirteen-year-old in junior high. But I might as well not have been there. Even though I know that I appeared at the school and even went through the onerous routine of English, history, math, I have only the dimmest memories of it, as if everything that occurred outside ballet happened on the other side of a scrim. Although I know its name—Montgomery Hills Junior High School—I don't remember what the school looked like, I don't remember ever entering it or leaving it, I have no precise memories of my courses or my academic teachers, and I can recall few encounters with anyone, especially anyone my own age, in its classrooms. I do remember endlessly doodling ballet positions, filling page after page with drawings of first position, second position, *passé*, *tendu*.

Gliding through school as if it didn't exist, waiting only to be released from its halls so that I could go to the studio, change into my practice clothes, and join my classmates at the barre—all that was changing me, leading me inexorably further and further from real life. The rupture between my ballet life and the life I was leaving behind became more and more apparent: I had no school friends, the telephone never rang for me, I was never invited to any school dances or parties, nor did it ever occur to me that I was missing anything or might want to go. My grades fell, even though I had always been a naturally good student without any effort. But when my grades plummeted (I have no memory of how low they were, or why—I suppose I just didn't care), my parents intervened.

Nor do I have any clear memory of their intervention, because even my parents in those heady years of my devotion to F. seemed flimsy and insubstantial, ghostly presences with barely an impact unless they aided or impeded my dancing. But they must have initiated *something*, because apparently there was a confrontation, some scene in which (possibly) they made demands and I was (probably) furious and coldly determined to ignore them—I hardly remember; it meant little to me. But the parental solution was that I was not to return to ballet school until my grades improved or my "attitude" improved or *something* improved that I hadn't the slightest interest in and no intention of either improving or changing in the least. I had every intention of disregarding school, disregarding my family; I intended to bolt from school at the afternoon's closing bell to rush to the studio, where I would claim my spot at the barre, coming home only when the ballet school closed for the night, well past family dinner hour. In that case, my parents must have said, they would no longer pay for my lessons. *Good,* I remember thinking. *Then I will run away from home, like Astrid.*

By the next day, it had dawned on me that I really was just some ordinary thirteen-year-old kid with no financial resources of her own. I hadn't realized it before but there *was* a monthly bill to pay. It galled me that I was still only a child, helpless, financially dependent. With no way to finance my lessons on my own, I would really have to quit. Or run away and join a ballet company, as Astrid had tried to do. If I were to stay at home with no ballet classes, attending school and doing my math and geography homework like a real person, life would be intolerable. *I would rather die,* I thought. At ballet school that day, before class, I sought out F., so desperate to tell him my plight that it never occurred to me that I had never before initiated a conversation.

Other people were milling around, but when I flagged down F. to talk he must have noticed how distressed I was. He immediately cleared a space for us to talk privately and, as if we were in his secret room, he concentrated entirely on me. I told him as simply as I could that I was in trouble at home and wouldn't be

permitted to come to class, that my parents were for-
bidding me to continue and would no longer pay for
lessons. I didn't explain why, and I didn't ask for anything, even for advice.

F. leaned in toward me, listening closely, but he
didn't say a word, didn't even ask me a single question. Then he looked at me in the hard focused way he
had when he was about to strike me, about to make a
mark.

"Your parents or me," he said abruptly when I had
finished my short explanation. "You have to choose."

I didn't ask any questions either.

"I choose you," I said.

Part 2

~ Partnering

*W*hen I told F., "I choose you," there was silence for a moment as we both thought over what I had said. I was stunned: I couldn't believe the words I had just heard myself saying. Yet I had no wish to take them back—the choice stood; I meant it. And F.?

"Then be *here*," F. answered suddenly, gesturing with a wide sweep of his arms all around us to the three studios where classes were going on and music was playing; to the lobby and the hallways where dancers were relaxing and lounging about, draped in chairs or on the floor, their towels around their necks, sewing ribbons to their pointe shoes or stretching in splits on the floor or vertically up the walls, all the while engaged in nonstop chatter. "Don't worry about the money," he continued, almost angrily, as if I might argue about it. "Just come. Every day." He turned his back and walked away.

So those were the terms. They didn't surprise me, not really. I knew what F. wanted, what he could easily elicit from me—the obedience, the dedication, the bravura performance even in class—and I knew the cost. I would be there every day, no matter what.

I had come so close to losing the dream F. instilled in me of becoming "a great dancer," so close to losing F. himself, the lyrical beauty of his classes and our hidden moments in his secret room, our glasses of schnapps raised to salute each other and cement our bond. But he had saved me, claimed me once again as his own, not—this time—with the brand of his cane on my inner thigh but with the demand to choose him over all others. To sever all other ties and be his, his own.

More than ever, I wished to be desirable to him; I even wanted to be desirable to myself, somehow, to take whatever was captivating about myself and enhance it, embellish it. To purify myself, to pare myself down to some formal essence of beauty—that was my goal, to achieve the tensile delicacy and fastidiousness that a life in ballet demanded. I hadn't yet learned to starve myself to thinness—I was too young, my body still childishly undeveloped—but I was working on my *inner* thinness, the devotion to ballet that pared away all the rest of life and kept it at bay.

Only a few years later, when I was no longer just a ballet *pupil*, a neophyte made ecstatically happy by a perfectly executed *échappé*, would I learn to live with hunger and to watch my friends in the ballet company survive on diets of carrots or sauerkraut. Later I would learn that when my ballet friends disappeared into the bathroom after a meal it was to force themselves to throw up while the rest of us darned our toe shoes and endlessly dissected our technique, our muscles and tendons and layers of fat, and our ever shifting rank within the company. Later I would recognize the peculiar, distinctive smell of anorexia and would know that when a girl's jawbones poked through her skin, looking like a fish spine around her mouth, and when her skin itself had that stretched, parched look of starvation, the rest of us were helpless to do anything. "Eat a milkshake!" we would plead in desperation. "Here, eat it!" But the starved girl wouldn't, or perhaps she couldn't, and we would end up pouring the milkshake down the sink in disgust. It was in those years, after F., that a girl named Margaret—my friend in the corps de ballet, whose hand I held in the *pas de quatre* in *Swan Lake* and who would lead the four of us cygnets haphazardly all over the stage unless I put pressure on her wrist and steered her as we danced—Margaret starved and vomited herself to emaciation while we watched and mostly ignored her, and when starvation didn't make her a better dancer, Margaret locked herself in and committed suicide. But Margaret's story would happen much later. In the years I was with F., unless F. fed me, I never thought about food.

I was hungry only for F., for the life he was offering me and preparing me for, for what he could give me. Whatever he could do for me—and to me—for that I was voracious. More and more I wanted F. to notice me constantly, not to be able to take his eyes from me no matter how ordinary and routine my exercises were; I wanted to prevent him from getting bored with just the ordinary loveliness of any girl working away at the barre and to keep his gaze fixed on me, to choose me over and over. When I was older and first saw dramatic ballets, like *Jardin aux Lilas* by Antony Tudor, in which each character has both a true love and a shadow lover, I thought, *Oh, yes, I danced this choreography with F.; the roles are familiar. In our ballet, I was the Young Girl in the virginal shift, possessed by the Older Man who circles around her, predatory and demanding, while off to the side is the Dark Wife making her futile gestures, ignored by everyone, smoldering.*

From F.'s conversation and the photographs he showed me in his secret room, I knew all about wives, how F. had been unhappy with them and had discarded them—two of them gone already. When F. was glum, I assumed it was because of a wife; when he was cheerful and funny, it was clearly because of me. *Sonya is no different from the other wives,* I thought pityingly, although she was F.'s youngest wife yet, and the most exotic.

Even when she had been my Intermediate teacher, I had paid little attention to Sonya, except to follow her instructions in class. I knew—all of us ballet girls knew—that her real job was to prepare us for F., that her class was just a way station en route to the pinnacle of Advanced Class with F., where, if we were lucky and gifted enough, we would undertake the serious work of becoming dancers. Once I entered F.'s orbit, with its lyrical, challenging classes ("dancy," we called them) and my clandestine visits to his secret room, I gradually saw Sonya differently—not only as a teacher or a mere third wife in a daisy-chain of wives, but as someone who years before might have been F.'s star student, his favorite. Someone, that is, like me. ("Watch out," Martine liked to warn me when F. was rude to Sonya or waved her off as if she didn't exist. "We're next in line.")

Had Sonya, when she was younger, met with F. in some earlier secret room, leaving wife number two on the sidelines teaching Intermediate girls? I imagined how attractive Sonya must have been as a young dancer, and how F. must once have been drawn to her dark beauty and flashes of sarcasm. She was glamorous even now, with black, kohl-rimmed eyes and glistening black hair tightly pulled back into a bun, as if the strands were glued to her head. But she also had the bulky body of the former dancer, with a rounded belly and calf muscles like tennis balls. Whenever she sat down she used both hands to stroke and knead her calves as if they were constantly cramped. Her leotard always seemed too tight, but Sonya did nothing to camouflage her bulges; rather she accentuated them with an elastic belt cinched tightly around her sturdy waist.

Even though she once had been F.'s student, Sonya had long ago lost any fear of F. and now sometimes seemed even to despise him. Tough and mercurial, she deferred ironically to F., as if to say that although he might once have been her teacher, now he was merely her husband—and not a very appealing one at that; she knew *his* game and wasn't about to put up with it. When he was in his worst, sulkiest, most mordant mood, she laughed flippantly at him and lit a cigarette, turning her back to him and shrugging him off. Then he would fume.

She smoked constantly to prevent herself from overeating, but really she liked nothing better than nibbling on chocolates. In the teachers' area of the school lobby, there was always a box of candy open on F.'s desk, each piece of chocolate wrapped invitingly in gold or silver foil. One of the ways that Sonya goaded F. into fury was to unwrap a chocolate slowly and eat it with relish; then it was *his* turn to turn his back, to make clear to everyone how bitter and disgusted he was, how burned up with irritation and gloom. But sometimes, if I were standing right there while his glamorous wife plucked a chocolate out of the box, F. would jump sharply at her, strike the candy from her hand, and then seize another from the box to hold out to me.

"You are thin, open your mouth," he would order angrily, tearing the foil from the chocolate and dropping it onto my tongue. Sonya would laugh mockingly at both of us and light another cigarette.

But I understood even then that it was not really my thinness that captivated F., that made him reward and prize me when Sonya irritated him. No, it was something else that must have drawn him to my side, some mix (that I imagined he saw so clearly in me) of brazen ambition and utter malleability. Sonya, whatever her past with F., was the finished product; I was still unformed, molten with ambitious yearning to be the great dancer I thought only F. could shape me into and for the career only he could forge. I was more like the ballerina in the photograph he showed me in his secret room, someone he could immobilize with one hand. Did it take the ballerina's breath away, as it did mine, to see F. crouch naked and wolflike beside her startled arabesque?

One day, to be "beautiful" and more sophisticated, I walked into class with a smudge of lipstick on and a light coating of mascara, in imitation of Astrid and the older girls. F. immediately pulled an immense white linen handkerchief out of his pocket, as if he were a magician unrolling a scarf to show that there was no rabbit in it, and with a great show of drama and involvement proceded to wipe my face with it while I continued my *battements tendus* at the barre. Neither of us missed a beat—I did my barre exercises, and he wiped and blotted away.

After that my mild interest in lipstick and mascara grew into a desire to apply enough makeup to my face to stock a drugstore, especially if it provoked F. The next day I repeated the applications, making both a shade lighter. F. stood in front of me while I was practicing at the barre, scrutinizing my face as if it were under a lamp, and then repeated his drama of the day before with the white handkerchief. I continued to act as if he were invisible. The next day I added eye shadow. When F. saw me he pointed to the door, telling me not to return until I had washed my face. I must have giggled, because my classmates looked at me stunned, startled (as I was) by my suppressed laughter, a sound never heard before or since in any ballet class I have ever experienced. Martine, standing next to me at the barre, flashed me a grin, not at all worried that her dab of eyeliner might be forbidden as well. F. just gazed at me sardonically, waiting for me to obey him and leave. So I trotted down to the girls' bathroom and wiped off the eye shadow with some toilet paper. Then we called a truce for a few days.

I gave in, that is, and went back to the scrubbed, mascaraless look that F. had ordained for me. But—I began to reason to myself—there was nothing *wrong* with makeup; I was certainly old enough to wear it, nor did it diminish my concentration or affect my *pliés* or pirouettes. Even Martine (I pointed out to myself) routinely wore her smudge of eyeliner to accentuate the Tartar slant of her dark eyes, and she was barely any older than I was. It didn't seem fair that I was the only one forbidden to try it. Makeup was just pretty, that was all. And it certainly got F.'s attention. So one day I spent a half hour before class not doing my usual warm-ups and stretches on the floor but sitting next to Astrid, in front of her mirror, carefully applying not only lipstick but eye shadow, liner, and swipes of mascara while she gave directions. Even a touch of rouge. Then I took my place at the barre.

F. strolled into class, dapper and whistling. He rapped with his cane against the floor, the music started, and we began our first-position *pliés*. It took only a moment or two for him to notice me, and then, without missing a beat or even interrupting the melodies of his whistling, he took me by both shoulders and propelled me out of class. Hands on my shoulders, he gamboled with me down the hall—still whistling, as if we were dancing a rakish pas de deux—and propelled me into the girls' bathroom and up to the sink. With a wave of queasiness and apprehension, I realized that F. had accompanied me into forbidden territory: It had never occurred to me that a boy, much less a grown man, would have the nerve to enter a girls' bathroom.

He turned on both taps as far as they would go, so

the water came flooding out in a great spray, bent me over the sink with one hand, and with his other splashed water all over my face, my hair, my neck, holding me under the water and soaking me. As soon as I started to choke and gasp for air, he let me up. Taking a wad of paper towels, he blotted and scrubbed my face.

"Close your eyes," he ordered, gently rubbing the eye shadow from my lids, and when the color didn't come off completely, he spit on a paper towel and rubbed again. Then he cupped my chin with one hand and just looked at me, looking at me hard and long with an amused, benevolent expression in his eyes. I waited, expecting something to happen—a slap? a kiss?—standing still, staring up at him, soaking wet, my eyelids and cheeks burning from the paper towels, but charmed and unafraid. I don't know why, but at that moment I felt thoroughly in love with him, as if he had showered me with gifts and I could reciprocate, give him gifts in return; we seemed to have made each other comically happy.

"Very pretty," he pronounced wryly, still holding me, looking into my eyes with his ironic half smile. "You don't need anything more."

But sometime later F. decided, seemingly on a whim, that without makeup and my face as unadorned as he had decreed, I was *not* pretty enough to please him entirely, and that therefore he would pierce my ears. If I wanted to look dazzling and sophisticated, so be it—I could wear earrings, gold studs or little gold hoops. All the other dancers had pierced ears, even Martine, whose ears had been pierced at birth, exotic Russian peasant that she was. Astrid's ears were pierced, too, of course: Any number of times I had sat next to her in her dressing room watching her in the mirror as she fiddled with her earrings. F. had pierced them for her, she told me proudly, but the importance of that information didn't sink in until the moment right before class, as we were all standing around waiting for the studio door to open, when F. beckoned me over and announced that now it was time for him to pierce mine.

My thoughts whirled for a second. I was strenuously afraid of needles and so tried to explain to F., politely of course, that I really preferred not to have my ears pierced quite yet. I was too young, I remonstrated, forgetting that only recently I had been trying to appear older; my parents would not allow it, I said firmly, even though F. and I both knew that my parents hardly saw me anymore. Even *I* recognized that those arguments would not avail. Truly I did not want holes in my ears, I continued: The very image made me queasy. I tried to laugh, to consider it a game, but the laugh was too forced, too anxious, too full of supplication for me to be let off. My polite refusals didn't work at all. Everyone's blood was up. While I watched with a kind of sickened fascination, F. called for a needle, some thread, a match. Is that all it took? Other people thronged around me as if part of the choreography, older dancers whom I hardly knew, girls and boys, laughing to themselves, reassuring me. "Don't worry," they said. "It won't hurt a bit; it only lasts a second."

F. signaled he was ready, but again I demurred. I was pushed down into a chair. Someone on either side of me held me down by the shoulders, and shoved my head back against the chair to keep it immobile. My arms were pinned to my sides. F. threaded the needle deftly, as if he were a seamstress, and passed it through the flame of a match to sterilize it. I recognized F.'s look: It was demonic and threw a kind of blackness between us, but everyone else was cheerful, even gay. I was on the edge of throwing up, passing out, or possibly dying, and wished only that one of these things would happen as soon as possible.

Suddenly, for no reason I will ever fathom, the laughter stopped, my arms were released, and I was let go. F. had changed his mind.

Even now, when I call up the image of myself in that chair, pinioned and fluttering like a trapped bird, with F. looming above me about to drill a hole in my earlobe, I can feel again the same trepidation: My body remembers the scratchy upholstery of the chair surrounding me, the pressure of the hands holding me down, how cold I was in the pit of my stomach. And yet I also remember a certain languor, as if my bloodstream had been flooded with barbiturates and I might, at any moment, drop off into a deep, passive sleep. To F. I must have looked drugged.

The odd thing was, even then he never touched me. When he held my face underwater and then scrubbed it with a paper towel, it was one of the few times he actually touched me with his own hands, out of ordinary human desire. It felt wonderful, like a caress. But when he was about to pierce my ears—and at the last moment refrained—or when he corrected me in class or in his secret room, he exerted his power over me without touch, almost without words, through his cane or with a sweep of his arm or a mere suggestive look. Glowing with forbidden makeup I could taunt him, it seemed; I could even lure him into the girls' bathroom as if that had been my intent all along. He in turn could have me imprisoned in a deep chair for his deft surgery—and so we danced back and forth in our choreographies of seduction and surrender.

As, for example, one day in class during adagio, that lovely, large, long unfolding of the body. We did it every day: adagio at the barre, when the suppleness of my own body and the slowness of the exercise kept me aware of F.'s every mood and deeply infatuated with him, with myself, with the measured, heavy beats of music vibrating under my hand on the barre. I could warm up my limbs and stretch them out, resting them on the particles of dust in the moist ballet air.

Adagio, done quickly and lightly, was usually relaxing, invigorating, but that day adagio was torture. F. had given us the simplest, most academic exercise: *développé en croix*, a term which itself is a kind of shorthand to mean that one does a slow, unfolding movement with the leg in a cross design—front, then side, then back, then side again. The moving leg goes very, very slowly, but high, to shoulder height or higher, while the rest of the body barely moves at all. These *développés en croix* were done to the pedantic rhythm of sixteen counts apiece, the slower the harder. I was tired.

The music started, the same old syrupy stuff, and I counted slowly to sixteen; it was one of those boring, tedious times when I seemed eternally parked at this barre. My mind wandered, and everything was painful. It wasn't often that I felt how agonizingly difficult these movements were; usually I was swept on by the beauty and discipline of the body, the controlled energy, the waves of music. The joy of dancing in class, of practicing, can be the simplest and most profound—how wonderful and exhilarating it is!—unsullied by performance, uncontaminated by an audience. But I was tired; I felt an uncontrollable lassitude.

F., as usual, prowled the studio. He seemed blithe, unconcerned, detached; as usual, he whistled. But he was often deceptive, really watching us the whole time. His detachment might be feigned to make us forget his presence, until, with a slight sardonic bow and a caustic insult, he would point out a mistake, an unforgivable error of placement or technique that only his exceedingly critical eye would catch. I had made constant private vows not to be caught off guard by that mixture of casual scrutiny and sardonic detachment.

But now I did it myself—I got careless. I forgot that F. was watching me; I forgot that, in truth, my desire was to ensure that he was my constant audience, that his gaze never left me. I who should have learned never to relax, never to think that any mistake of mine would be ignored, who did everything to remain in F.'s spotlight, I was too tired to be vigilant. So when F. walked by me while I was doing the adagio, while I was in *développé à la seconde*, with my leg stretched out to the side at just about the height of my shoulder, I was at first conscious of placing everything perfectly, so that F. would pass me by without comment. Once he moved on, however, my strength lapsed. I wilted. Instead of completing the adagio, holding my *développé* in place in the air and filling out all sixteen murderous counts, I simply gave myself a little forbidden assistance and tucked my hand under my ankle.

Without anything having changed in the room, I

understood immediately that I had committed a fatal error: I was "cheating," the cardinal sin of ballet, and F. knew it. Instead of continuing his progress around the class, F. must have turned around and caught me—I knew this with utter certainty although nothing had happened. Although he was well behind me and I could not see him at all, I sensed that the whole studio of dancers vibrated with the awareness that F. was furious, livid, white-hot with anger, and I had provoked it. Then I didn't dare to release my ankle for fear of acknowledging that I should not have lazily cheated in the first place. It was as if a shutter had snapped inside my head, and there I was, frozen for all time, caught in the act.

I waited; I knew I was in for it. And I was right—the cane came down across my arm, then across my leg. "Stay," F. commanded from right behind me. "Don't move." He was close enough for me to feel him, whispering in my ear with immediate and intense courtesy, and while I did not dare to move a fraction, an eyelash, my whole body began to tremble. Gently the stick traveled over my body, tapping here and there, almost caressing me—touching my shoulders, elbows, buttocks, thighs, and now everything was just where it should be, pulled high and clean, a perfect *développé à la seconde*. I could hear F. breathing behind me, smell the strong scent of cigarette, feel his warmth as he touched me. Everything was perfect except that I was shaking uncontrollably.

Torture works; all dancers know this.

So dancers covet violence as a gift. Not only does it jolt you a fraction closer to the perfection of ideal form, it is the very moment—the sharp, transient moment—of intimacy. While violence might be forbidden in mundane, heavy-limbed real life, for a dancer it takes on a breathtaking sweetness; a dancer can't get enough of it. Such attention proves that your promise is beyond that of the others—you are cherished, beloved. When F. stood so close behind me, enveloping me with the heat of his presence and staying close enough to whisper his commands into my ear, it felt seductive, inviting: In front of the whole class, while my body shook delicately but uncontrollably, F. was showing me the sweet tenderness of possible lovemaking, laced with the palpable, sharp thrill of danger.

Little by little I began to realize that other girls were jealous of me. "F. never corrects *me*," my friends would say to me bitterly after class as we changed back into our street clothes. "He looks only at *you*." The girls were right; I didn't even make a pretense of arguing. F. was generally oblivious—even callously indifferent—to anyone but the one dancer he favored, so I could only nod at my friends in abashed agreement, sorry for them but pleased for myself as if F., in striking me or embarrassing me with a particularly barbed insult, had instead been pasting stars all over my report card. Not only had F. singled me out as the object of his attention but, as we all realized, his brutality worked: If he struck my leg it went up higher, straighter, like an arrow or a comet; when he hurled insults at my *fouettés* they picked up speed and precision; when he stalked me through the class or stridently banged the floor with his cane during our large jump combinations, my *grands jetés* lifted farther into the air, stretched wider in splits. Any one of us would have died for that attention.

In my ballet class were twins whose names not only rhymed—Stacy and Tracy—but who were exact replicas of each other, with beautiful blue eyes, dark lashes, and long thick dark hair plaited in two braids. Both of them initially were my friends: Together we'd pull on our practice clothes in the girls' dressing room, lounge around chatting at the door to the studio before class, sometimes stand next to each other at the barre. But I could feel the twins becoming more and more despondent over the intensity of care that F. lavished on me. I could feel them pulling away from me, making alliances with the other girls, beginning to look at me differently, as if because F. had singled me out I could no longer be their friend.

Finally they quit the class. One of the twins came to me and announced ceremoniously, "We're leaving. Because of you. You get all the attention." She wasn't being vindictive; she was merely explaining to me what had been clear for some time. I looked at her and nodded, understanding perfectly. I had nothing to say because her analysis was entirely true. F. had isolated me; I devoured all his attention.

Ballet is Darwinian: The fittest flourish and the others quit. Those not talented or driven enough to succeed are ignored, made to feel invisible. Perhaps their bodies bulge in the wrong places, or their muscles are not pliant enough, or their proportions don't match the template of whatever is the current physiognomic ideal for a ballerina—they leave. If the dancer doesn't figure out these drawbacks for herself, she is finally told by her teachers that she has "no future," and with barely a wave and no hearty encouragement she is out the door. Friendly farewells are for real people, not for dancers. Stacy and Tracy understood soon enough that they were caught in a merciless system that would label them failures, so they did the intelligent thing and bowed out early, probably with their semester's lessons all prepaid. I was sure they were not entirely sorry to leave the ballet world, having already tasted its merciless humiliations.

When the twins left ballet school to return to their real lives, they seemed to be going to a country far away, one I had once visited myself but now could barely remember. Having only the faintest idea of ordinary life, I imagined that with their sturdy bodies, beautiful blue-violet eyes, and long braids, Stacy and Tracy would be "normal" teenage girls. Their real life (as I imagined it) would include teenage boys, that commodity the ballet world values about as highly as sunshine, another lethal substance that might turn a wraithlike ballet girl into a suntanned sweetheart. So I pictured Stacy and Tracy marching directly from our girls-only ballet class to an unknown but benign world of cheerleaders and junior-high rock 'n' roll, with boyfriends in math class, boyfriends on the phone, boyfriends in cars who would drive them after school to the local Hot Shoppe for hamburgers and milkshakes. I knew I would miss the twins' friendship in the dressing room, but I had long ago accepted the cost: I would lose friends, even ballet friends, but I would gain F. There would be no boyfriends, no dates at the Hot Shoppe, but the older man I adored would fix his ironic gaze on me, work his will on my body.

And he would tend me, too, like an affectionate mother lion licking one cub while bringing the rest of the pack into line. Quick as he was with his cane, he would sweetly, almost absentmindedly, hold my wrist during barre exercises, all the while snarling insults at the rest of the class as if they were tumbling gracelessly at his feet and I were the only one behaving properly. When he had finished berating all of them, he would turn back to me and pat my hand a few times as if to say, "Don't get discouraged. You and I are in this together." Or there would be a wink and a quick pinch on the cheek.

So it was unthinkable for me to do anything but stay with F. My life—like that of all dancers—was rich in oxymorons: submissive power, obedient mastery. If I thought about F. standing so close behind me that he could easily have wrapped his arms around my waist, whispering in my ear and using his cane to touch every part of my body, the neurons of my brains would lurch and spin as if I were prey to powerful charges of electrical current. He bewitched me with contradictions, making me tremble with fear and yet feel myself in utter control, as if I surged with power. "It"—the object I called my body, the supple machine that was a ballerina in training—that object was shared by both of us, and we worked on it, shaped it, together; it was as much F.'s as my own.

When torture didn't succeed in making us spin faster, kick higher, or stay in the air longer, it satisfied the cravings instilled in us by ballet codes to "do anything," brave any terror, suffer any deprivation for ballet. If Martine did badly in class, she punished herself afterward at home by walking around in new pointe shoes without any protective lambswool until her toes bled. Only then would she take off her shoes. When she described this self-mutilation to me, I agreed with her that it was a good idea.

I remember doing splits against the doorjamb of my bedroom, stretching my leg straight up the wall and then pressing my body against it. But that was nothing. Sitting in my bedroom with my heels together, trying to press my knees to the floor, was harder. When I couldn't quite get my knees all the way down, I dragged over a heavy piece of furniture and tried to position it on one knee, holding it down, so that I could use all my strength to press down the other one. But I still couldn't get both knees to the floor: No piece of movable furniture that I could pull on top of me and place over my leg was heavy enough to weight my knee to the floor and hold it there. All I could do was force the stretch with my hands, using all my strength.

The stretch was so painful it made me cry, or perhaps I was crying out of the sheer desire to torture myself, to inflict pain on myself, to pull my muscles beyond where they wanted to go. Maybe I cried from frustration that I couldn't hurt myself enough.

"It's supposed to hurt," we would say like a litany, shoving and pummeling each other's recalcitrant limbs into one extreme position after another, while the girl being stretched would gasp for breath and submit. The desire for perfection—and its utter inachievability—endlessly drove us, even when we could barely breathe or our faces had gone white in agony. The more pain we could endure, the more exalted we felt. Afterward we weren't even limp; we seemed stronger, ready for more.

Before class we would lie on the floor of the studio stretching our muscles and cracking the vertebrae of our spines one by one, fingering each individual tendon, bone, and ridge. We wrapped our legs in Saran Wrap and wore latex baby pants beneath our leotards to sweat away fat from our hips and thighs, so that when we finally unwrapped and undressed we were bathed in perspiration, rivers of it, from the waist down. We hairpinned velvet bows or artificial flowers around our chignons and learned never to grimace, no matter how stabbing the pain.

Once in class we dancers always had the mirror, a giant reflecting sheet covering one entire wall; we would rarely take our eyes from it. Just as I tracked Astrid's gaze in her dressing room mirror even though I was sitting right next to her on a bench with our shoulders practically touching, dancers watch themselves in the mirror all day long. Other than one's teacher—who might be as quixotic as F., noticing every detail or, just as likely, ignoring the dancers entirely for days on end for some private, moody obsession—the mirror is the one constant presence in every dancer's life.

Gazing all day long into the studio mirror has a hypnotic and calming effect, like the pink walls modern penal theory recommends as a cell color to calm the tempers of the most violent inmates. Put a ballerina in front of a mirror, and she will instantly get the glazed, inward look of a devotee of a cult; her body will start turning slowly, rotating from side to side as if strung on a plumb line, and the slight, ritual pawings of the feet will automatically begin. But the eyes will never leave their fixed point on the mirror. In Jerome Robbins's ballet *Afternoon of a Faun*, the audience itself is the imaginary mirror-wall for two young dancers falling in love. The girl is so entranced by herself that even when the boy finally, tentatively, kisses her, she never, not even then, looks away from her reflection. Like the girl in the ballet, what we cared for most was what we saw in the mirror.

Yet seductive as the mirror was, it was not meant to reward us. Rather it threw back at us an ever changing image of flaws to correct. The checklist was infinite. Right hip slightly raised. Fourth position too open. Too closed. Pirouette off. Leg not straight in arabesque. Shoulder. Elbow. Fingers. The tilt of the head. Wider. Cleaner. Sharper. Higher. With a mirror we could catalog every misplaced hair, every shred of kinetic error, every kilowatt of misdirected energy. Somewhere hidden in the mirror was the perfection we all searched for, whereas on its scrim—what we could actually see—was only deviation and error.

Not that any of us minded—after all, we were all there for a purpose, not to be stripped of identity but to refashion another one, a classically organized form beyond the grasp of ordinary mortals. The music surged through the barres, through our bodies, someone called out counts, the air was dense and heavy with sweat, and we glided away in our *glissades* and *pas de bourrées*, doing what we loved best. What we gave up the world for.

One day I was dancing about, enjoying myself, entranced with myself, the music, my talent, the little loveliness of the choreographic tchotchkes we did daily in class. *Malenkie quelques choses*, F. called these dances in Russian-French, "little nothings," even when they were fiendishly difficult.

That day there was only thunderous, moody silence from F. Then an accusation: I am looking in the mirror at my face—of all things!—enjoying the way I look, not watching for my flaws and errors, indeed not paying attention to them at all, but simply gazing at how pretty I am. Warily I apologize.

But my muttered "Sorry" wasn't enough, or perhaps I was not sorry enough to satisfy F. One could not remove the mirror, so instead F. instructed me to turn around completely, to continue the class facing the back wall. Worse, not only was I turned 180 degrees, but so was the entire class, all of them presumably blameless but nevertheless victims of my self-love.

We were all forced to continue in this awkward situation for a month, a month of daily disorientation. Each day, hoping for a reprieve and not getting one, we collectively sank further into depression; my classmates sent me evil looks, poured silent hatred on me for my criminal vanity. When F. finally allowed us to face the mirror again and I happened to catch a quick, forbidden glimpse of my face, a little shudder of guilt and fear ran through me, a little Pavlovian electroshock. I immediately realized that F. was completely right: I loved to look at myself. I suddenly saw myself as I truly was: thirteen years old and devastatingly beautiful.

After that F.'s accusation became overwhelmingly true—all I wanted was to examine myself minutely in the mirror, from every angle, with complete absorption. I was totally enraptured. Even when I moved awkwardly, when I made mistakes or did something stupidly wrong, even when I was so out of breath that I grabbed the barre and gasped for air, my chest heaving, I was compellingly beautiful. I was mesmerized; I knew that I could gaze at myself all day. The more I was forbidden to look, the more I wanted to see. "Do you see how beautiful you are?" he had asked, and yes, I saw what he saw, the beauty of my body moving through the "little nothings" F. gave us to perform.

F.'s immediate reaction to my every look and gesture—from how I gladly flaunted my forbidden makeup to the way my eyes locked onto my own image in the mirror—propelled me always deeper into that narcissism so characteristic of dancers. *He loves me,* I thought, and I surely in turn adored him, as if I were the sinuous clay he could repeatedly fashion and refashion, neither of us ever tiring of it. What seemed to enchant F. and keep him at my side, holding my wrist or hovering behind me in near embrace, was my volatile, in-between state of *becoming*—I was a girl becoming a woman, becoming "a great dancer," but still his pupil, still a child, as if he could fix me forever in time, unchanged.

I see now that F. must have loved women—not real women in their full-blown adulthood, but girl-women, a girl as I was, just tipping over into woman-hood. In the ballet world, full blooming womanhood is not prized. So F. kept me fresh and unadorned, a half doll whom he could feed and whose limbs he could manipulate, who never rebuffed him or cried and who looked to him for everything. He mothered me and fathered me: In the midst of a family of sisters who changed into practice clothes with me in the dressing room, stood next to me at the barre, lined up with me at the water fountain after class, the center of my world was always F., nourishing me with his constant, unremitting attention. His every gesture made my pulse hum. When I told F. "I choose you," what I really meant was, "No one but you."

When I try to recall what else I did in those days, how I spent my time when I wasn't in ballet class or in F.'s secret room, aware of his every mood and motion, I have one image from real life that persists in my memory—buses. Long rides on them. One bus after another. I left school, took a bus to a transfer point, took another bus, possibly even another one after that, until I came to a place that nowadays I recall only in dreams, a cement island in the middle of a busy intersection called, in my dream, "Sixteenth and Calvert." Whether the place really existed I have no idea, but the end point, certainly, was the ballet school. More precisely, my daily class with F. At night I would reverse the order: bus after bus to a depot, and then one final bus out to my home. Often it was late, well after rush hour, even after dark, so my rides would be almost solitary, and the depot would be darkened, often deserted except for me. If I missed my late bus I would have to sit in that darkened, empty waiting room on a wooden bench until the next bus arrived.

Those were the worst moments—hours, really—for me: the darkness and solitude, the transition between the ballet studio and home. Those were the only times I ever thought, *I am too young. F. isn't enough for me. I need a mother or a father.* But I wouldn't allow myself to call them, to ask them to come for me and bring me home: I had made a choice in one moment, a clear and direct choice for F., for the freedom to become a dancer at whatever the price, and had no right now to ask others to take care of me, no matter how lonely I felt. I almost never nowadays dream of F., rarely even of dancing, but often of those darkened buses, of being alone on a bus or in a bus station, waiting, carrying my dance case full of practice clothes and Jean Naté, not having any idea of how long I will be traveling on those buses, hour after hour, always alone.

At the end of my first year with F. in Advanced, I was promoted again, along with Martine, to the next level. It was still called "Advanced" but tacitly known to the dancers, as aware of arcane distinctions as any kabalist, to be the level where one's aspirations might possibly lead out of the classroom and onto the stage.

For the first time our class included boys, a species before now trained separately and thus excluded from our female universe—ballet boys, that is, not real boys who in my imagination were busy courting Stacy and

Tracy. These ballet boys were a little older and not much taller than we were, boys dressed identically in black tights and white T-shirts, their hair slicked back and their faces newly shaved. "The boys," as we called them, were nameless, interchangeable, and as different from us as zebras or puppies. They paid no attention to us, and we in turn dismissed them as interlopers in our all-girls world, and clumsy interlopers at that. We were stronger, swifter, more polished than they; they were both softer and gawkier than we, as if their muscles hadn't yet been fully developed and their bodies were not yet under their full control. No one wanted to stand next to them at the barre, but when it was the boys' turn to dance in the center, we girls lined the barres and watched them carefully. In their awkward, unformed way they could sometimes jump higher than we could or spin out more turns, even if sometimes they stumbled or crash-landed into a wall.

F. took a warm but ironic interest in the boys and was sometimes unsettlingly jocular, as if he and they were all together in a fraternity, with F. in charge of hazing. He even told them jokes that we girls couldn't overhear, making them erupt with laughter until he banged on the floor with his cane to get them back to work. When we did *grands jetés* across the studio, F. would drag a bench to the middle of the floor for the boys to leap over as if they were horses clearing a hurdle, or, like a ringmaster in a circus, he would urge them on by whipping his cane through the air to the sounds of forceful whistling. He had his chosen one among the boys, as with the girls, making demands on his favorite and offering suggestions with a grim, manly determination. He "corrected" that boy, too— the promising one—once hitting him so hard we could hear the stroke across the room, making all the rest of us flinch. "So you will remember," F. told him, just as he had often said to me.

After class he had the boys doing push-ups and lifting weights. "For heavy ballerinas," he would say out of the side of his mouth, pantomiming how a man might be called on to hoist one into the air. "Whew!" he would say, wiping imaginary sweat from his brow.

"Pansies," Martine would whisper to me, fluttering her wrists and languidly closing her slanted eyes whenever the boys did something awkward. "Fairies." Martine approved of real boys, not ballet boys; she met them at school and told me about them later in the dressing room—real boys who bought six-packs and drove around in Volkswagens or old Chevy convertibles. Real boys who tried to feel her up, Martine said, laughing at what they found—the hard muscles and stringy sinews of her dancer's body. Our bodies were no surprise to us; after all, we dancers felt each other up all the time. But once she persuaded me to attend a party with her, where I encountered thickets of sweaty boys drinking beer and lurching into girls who giggled and tried to grab the bottles away. It made me uneasy that a dancer—even one as bold as Martine—would enjoy such unballetic company, and I was relieved when Martine checked her watch and returned us to her house in time for curfew and bed.

Despite Martine's tutelage, whatever real boys and girls might do in a normal life was vague to me, even though I was still putting in a few hours a day at a regular school, crowding my academic subjects into the mornings. Then I headed straight for the ballet school and class with F., carrying my high-energy lunch of hard-boiled eggs, bread, cheese, dried apricots, and candy bars in plastic sandwich bags, while the other, real teenagers stayed behind to line up raucously (or so I imagined) for spaghetti in the school cafeteria. But the activities on which my classmates spent all their seemingly endless free time were completely foreign to me. Apparently they put on shorts and sneakers to race around the gym doing sports; they participated in after-school clubs like French Club or Chess Club or Photography; they went out on dates, talked to one another on the phone at night, listened to "greatest hits" while I was listening to Chopin, Czerny, Scriabin, and Tchaikovsky surging through the humid, resin-filled air of the ballet studio.

Curious about real boys and not wanting to rely on Martine, I allowed myself—with some embarrassment, as if I were doing something perverse—to acquire what other girls my age might have called a boyfriend. His name was Danny, and he didn't know a thing about ballet. Instead he was interested in math and science and was the most studious boy I had come across, not that I was well acquainted with other students or paid much attention to our shared classwork. Danny, for his part, seemed delighted by me, and amiably put up with a girl who had little time for him and no comprehension of his life.

Except that he wasn't a dancer, Danny was easy to like, with his sweet humorousness, his intelligence, and the generosity of his attention to me. Now, instead of my dressing-room talks with Astrid and my timid foray into boy/girl partying with Martine, I could talk about "life" with Danny, to discover what it was that real boys did and thought about, boys who were different from the ones Martine knew but still worlds away from the ballet boys flinging themselves at F.'s urging into double *sauts de basques* and leaping over benches in class.

It turned out that what Danny thought about a great deal, other than math problems, was my body ("So what else is new?" Martine said when I confided in her), but, to his quiet disappointment, I barely noticed *his* body and wasn't remotely interested in it. Danny was not even as strong as I was—he was frail, as if he were much younger, thinner and less muscular than I, and even less muscular than the ballet boys lifting weights and doing push-ups at F.'s direction. Danny couldn't have lifted me even an inch from the ground, and I was hardly a "heavy ballerina." I knew his weaknesses full well because, at his instigation, we had tried a little clumsy partnering: He would clasp his hands lightly around my waist with about the same force as one would use to hold an ice cream cone, I would count to three and jump, immediately landing right back where I had started. *"Hold me!"* I would demand, tightening his hands around my waist, but he couldn't; he was afraid he would hurt me. He thought I was fragile, breakable. I considered myself indestructible.

So what Danny and I usually did together (on my rare day off from ballet practice or a late Sunday afternoon) was a quick shared round of math homework punctuated by tentative gropings on his part—not even for a kiss (I don't think we ever kissed) but for a sort of brushing up against each other or, unbidden, a warm hug that consisted of his pulling me to him tightly and then letting me go, just as quickly. The touching didn't interest me much; it seemed too tentative to make an impact on either of us. I wasn't used to such diffuse and undirected touching; when I was touched by someone at the ballet school it was always in a specific place and for a specific purpose. "Tighten *that*," F. would say, drawing a horizontal line with his finger from one shoulder blade to another, or, "Pull up here. Straighten your leg." But what Danny wanted to do, it seemed, was just to touch me any-where, or all over, with no particular goal except for the sensation.

The other kind of touching he wanted, something he seemed to find terribly forbidden, was to spank me, especially if he could find some specific rationale for it, such as a badly worked-out math problem. He would swat at me through my clothes, and once, in a risky moment, lifted my skirt (out on the street! in public!) and gave me a gentle slap I could barely feel through my slip and underpants. It made me laugh.

To guide me toward what he assumed I knew nothing about, Danny gave me a book about sexuality, handing it to me in the same determined but slightly furtive way that F. in the secret room handed me the photograph of himself partnering his ballerina. Danny's contraband was a textbook, with diagrams and euphemistic suggestions about "trust" and how "a man and wife" could "make each other feel special," but all the book taught me was that relationships out-side the ballet world must be utterly tame, with no allure at all. Not all the diagrams in the book or even its "Appendix of Deviant Sexuality"—with such head-ings as "Coprophilia," "Foot Fetishism," "Necrophilia," "Sodomy"—could teach me as much about special-ness as that one photograph of F. aggressively naked and crouching like a wolf at the foot of his ballerina, his one hand immobilizing her in arabesque. Could a boyfriend or a husband from the real world bring me as much pleasure and excitement as F. did? Cherish, correct, and feed me? Pin me in a chair to pierce my ears? Summon me to a secret room where anything could happen? Could anyone but F. create a universe of music, of bodies glistening with sweat, of perfect form? Shape a girl into a great dancer?

I knew that within hours of math homework with Danny I would be back in the ballet world, where anything was possible. Only there would I surrender, at my own desire, to a man who had license to touch me anywhere and who ruled over me with a suggestive look and a readiness to inflict pain. A man whom I could charm with a smile or drive into a controlled frenzy when I simply relaxed an elbow or fell off a pirouette. Or when I looked at him insolently. Or when I had a good time, ignoring him altogether. I knew that it was only F.—with his sardonic comments or a quick flick of his cane or his way of tipping my head back to slosh a drink down my throat—only F. who engendered my trust, who could make me "feel special."

One day as we were all heading for the door after class, F. whistled—not one of his endlessly inventive dance melodies but a few short blasts, like a policeman's, to get our attention. I turned around. With another sort of whistle that meant "Come on," F. motioned to me to return with him to the empty studio.

"Time," he said matter-of-factly when the other dancers had closed the door behind them and we were alone, "to learn pas de deux." I nodded, uncertain of how I might "learn pas de deux" when not a single ballet boy was in sight.

Not even noticing my acquiescence, F. put a record on a phonograph, switched on the machine, and lowered the needle with unerring accuracy to the few bars just before the pas de deux from *Les Sylphides*. Motioning me to his side, he jammed his cigarette in his mouth and with both hands wordlessly arranged my body in the ballerina's pose with my own hands lightly held together near my face and my head tilted toward him. *"Sauté arabesque,"* he said quietly as the music started, the cigarette dangling from the side of his mouth. All of a sudden with that first jump I was lifted into the air, posed in arabesque, his hands around my waist. It was the strangest sensation, being held aloft by F.: He kept me there for a moment, and then without any help from me lowered my body slowly back to the floor, sliding me all the way down his chest.

"Not so much force," he admonished me when I was back on the ground. "I could do you with one hand." I fully believed he could, and thought he might demonstrate this feat as in the photograph with the ballerina. Yes, he could certainly do me with one hand; he had often done so. With his cigarette still dangling from the side of his mouth, he told me the choreography that came next, then fleetingly danced the steps himself to show me where they should go and to have me envision the quicksilver lightness of the *Sylphide* style. Lean and sinewy as he was, casually dressed in khaki trousers and a loose white cotton shirt, smoking away, he nonetheless made an exquisite sylph.

F. dropped the phonograph needle again at the same place on the record, and we began again. "Easy *up!*" he warbled, lifting me again into the air in arabesque, holding me in space for a moment, and lowering me down so slowly that I barely even felt it as I touched the floor with the tip of my pointe shoe.

Because it was my first time airborne at any partner's hands, the sensation of the lift was the most astonishing: I felt weightless, defying gravity as I stayed in the air, but also immensely heavy, blocklike, as if I were a weighty object thrust upward as one would fork up a bale of hay or hoist a bag of cement. It was only much later, when I had done these lifts hundreds of times, that I realized the strength a man must have, not so much to lift the woman—because on the way up the woman adds her own force—but to lower her gently back down to the floor, instead of, as dancers say, dropping her like a sack of potatoes. I learned that once I left the ground it was entirely F.'s power and his hands on me that kept me aloft. The timing was critical: It took only a misstep or two to learn that I had to be synchronous with F., to learn his rhythms and to pace myself.

With him, I was completely without embarrassment, letting F. touch me in a way no man had ever touched me before, his hands encircling my rib cage, feeling the solidity and warmth of his body as I flew up and was gently lowered against his chest back to the ground, wafting up and floating down entirely at his behest. I half expected F. to pant mockingly and wipe his brow of imaginary sweat. But he was tender to me, fun loving, bemused at my awkwardness, teasing me by holding me in the air a second longer than I expected, pressing my body to his chest to slow my descent. His body was warm, he hadn't burned me with his cigarette, and his bow tie was slightly askew. I loved that: that he was disheveled.

A day or two later F. whistled to me again to keep me after class but this time instead of *Les Sylphides* on the phonograph he had two older boys for me: Chico, a dark, stocky Spaniard, and Ivan, a tall Russian. At F.'s direction Ivan grasped me by my left ankle and my left wrist, swung me into the air and flew me around and around in circles, as if I were a toy airplane. F. signaled with a whistle, Chico reached out for me as I flew by, and with hardly a break in the speed of my flight I was passed off to Chico, this time held by my right ankle and right wrist. And so it went: Chico and Ivan passed me back and forth, swooping me around and around, up and down, making waves in the air. All I had to do was keep my arms and legs outstretched, my body rigid, my head up. All I had to do was not look down at the floor, not get scared. "Getting used to it?" F. inquired of me when the boys slowed down and deposited me in an awkward bundle back on the floor.

After that Ivan, Chico, and I practiced daily when our regular class was over and everyone else had been dismissed to the dressing room. Martine, who was more experienced than I, also joined us, and then F. made up ever more complicated routines for the boys to fly us around the studio and toss us in all directions, spinning us in the air to the music of Scriabin. As we all became more adept, F. began to teach us the choreography for Glazunov's *Four Seasons* with its grand *bolshoi* lifts and swoops in the air. I learned how to do supported pirouettes, when the man simply puts both hands on your waist and spins; I practiced fish dives, involving a leap into a man's arms and then a dip to the floor; and we did endless finger turns. From the audience's point of view, a finger turn looks elegant and almost effortless, but what is happening is that the woman grasps the man's middle finger, held over her head, and pivots herself around that imaginary vertical pole.

I learned repeatedly in these sessions that two bodies can be more intimate than I had ever imagined.
The man will touch and explore his partner's sinews,
her ribs, her hipbones, even more assiduously than a
dancer might touch herself, as he looks for a finger-
hold, a hard-muscled place to hold on to. If the folds
of my skin inside my leotard were soft, F. would pinch
it as if to say, *Get rid of this; no one could hold on to you
here.*

Sometimes the body betrays itself, too, in ways that
I hadn't foreseen. Watching the boys practice with
Martine, I saw her slide off Chico's shoulder, where
she was perched in arabesque, leaving a trail of blood
on the sleeve of his white T-shirt. Neither of them
said a word about the stain but continued to practice
as if nothing had happened; Martine's nonchalance
left me awestruck. Sometime earlier Martine had
taken me in hand to prevent just such an accident: My
mother, when I had gotten my first period, had given
me a packet of sanitary pads and what looked like a
garter belt to hold them—it was this cumbersome
arrangement Martine had discovered one day beneath
my leotard. "You can't wear *that*!" she had said, and
took me to the girls' bathroom, where she unwrapped
what looked like a paper cylinder. After taking it apart
and instructing me in its use, she handed me a new
one and pointed me toward a stall. "You can buy yourself a box later," she said, "with directions and dia-

grams inside, but for right now, just find the hole and put it in." When I wailed from inside the stall (a disciplined and quiet wail; after all, we were dancers) that I would hurt myself, Martine would have none of it. "Shut up," she ordered. "You can't possibly hurt yourself. You don't even have a cherry anymore—what do you think all that stretching does to you?" Martine was right, of course. I immediately converted to her method. But seeing her leave a visible track on Chico's shirt made me realize just how palpably dangerous this new partnering might turn out to be.

Sweat, too, caused dangers I had never thought about. After a few minutes at the barre, for example, most dancers are glistening, and after thirty minutes they are dripping wet, leaving little pools of sweat on the floor around them and on the barre under their hands. Doing pirouettes, *fouettés*, or *chaîné* turns in the center, dancers give off a spray of sweat, like a sprinkler suddenly spurting. I quickly learned with Ivan and Chico that we all had to towel off first so that the boy could grip me firmly; there were times when one of the boys would pull me to him but we were both so wet and slick that I would slide out of his grasp like a wet fish. Once I was asked to leap from a lying-down position on the floor to Ivan's shoulder, but when he pulled and I jumped we both were so glazed with sweat that our bodies slid right past each other. Soaring right over his shoulder like a fish yanked on a line, I landed with a thud on the floor behind him.

The hardest lift for me, though, was one in which, at F.'s signal, I had to run headlong at Ivan, who would grab my pelvis with both hands and thrust me over his head, where, high in the air, I would arch myself into the shape of a bird. The first few times we tried the lift I missed it entirely, dashing panic-stricken out of Ivan's reach, or, worse, wilting halfway up to the top, so that Ivan had no choice but to drop my limp body back onto the floor. The first time I made it all the way up over Ivan's head I was exultant. But also sickly terrified, as if I had swooped into a realm of diminished oxygen and were paddling precariously in ether while my body—my real, earthy, sensate body—remained rooted to the ground. With jolts of dizziness, I remembered that Ivan was more than six feet tall. From far below I could hear F.'s voice.

"Stay up there," F. was saying. "Don't come down."

He seemed miles below me, his voice the merest echo. When I glanced downward I could see him, distorted as from a great distance; I saw that he was looking up at me and holding his cane out in front of him, touching it at both ends with the tips of his fingers, flexing it ever so slightly. He was sending me a signal that needed no more words. If I came down, he was telling me, I would regret it.

Obediently, and with a certain thrill despite my dizziness, I arched my back, arched my neck, tilted my

chin upward to the ceiling, stretched my arms outward as far as they would go. High in the studio ether,
I rested regally, my pelvis held tightly in Ivan's large
hands, his fingers welded to the curve of my bones.
Holding me aloft at F.'s direction, Ivan casually
strolled with me around the studio, at every few steps
almost banging me headlong into the fluorescent
lights. Every now and again, he would notice a light
fixture in my path and bend his knees; we both
dipped.

But it was really F. who kept me up in the air, even
though I could feel the strength of Ivan's hands circling my body. The thrill of F.'s threat, the knowledge
that I was slicing through the air at his behest only,
kept me aloft as surely as if I had wings. I wouldn't
have dreamed of asking to be let down, even though a
careless step of Ivan's would have smashed my face
into the lights. I knew that if I were to relax my body
for the merest instant, it would drop limply around
Ivan's hands and a second later I would be unceremo-
niously dumped on the floor. So I focused into the far
distance, into the beyond, the nowhere, the space
dancers look into when in fact they are blinded by
stage lights and can see nothing. I stared steadily into
space, imagining I was onstage, doing a real pas de
deux in front of an audience.

Either Ivan tired of holding a hundred pounds over
his head, roaming around the studio with the dead

weight, or F. nodded permission to him to end our practice, so he slowly brought me down, sliding one hand along my chest and his other hand under my outstretched leg until I lightly touched the floor in arabesque.

Later I found Ivan's fingerprints on my body, his thumbs etched into my stomach and his fingers spanning my hips, each bruise distinct. The marks on my body reminded me of the thin welt left by F.'s cane on my first day in his class, each print on my flesh an insignia sealing me further into the ballet world. No matter who actually touched me—whether it was Ivan or some other boy—the fingerprints were F.'s; when I saw myself naked it was F.'s "handwriting" I always recognized.

But after that first pas de deux from *Les Sylphides*, F. himself never partnered me again, although I would have been happy, overjoyed, if the lesson with him had gone on forever. I realized, though, in those few moments alone in the studio with F., that he was teaching me something beyond choreography: He was bequeathing me, as a gift, my first sensation of what to do when a man's hands are around you, where you tighten, where you relax, at what point you gather all your own strength and give aid, at what point you surrender and let him do everything. F.'s gentle strength, his control of the pace and trajectory of my body in the air, his hands under my ribs, coupled with the exquisite lightness of his own mimed dancing of the woman's role and his slightly self-amused irony—all of that instantly became for me the essence of pas de deux. Even more than that, in the partnering of the older man and the young girl I could feel in my body that love (or so I saw it) that kept us in the studio alone that day, the yearning on my side to please him and to give my body over to his control, and, on his, the sweet and earnest attentiveness.

But as if those moments lifting me in the air had been *too* tender, *too* intimate, F. would never repeat them, not with his own hands on me. Instead he would nod to one of the boys or let out a short whistle—then Ivan or Chico would grasp my waist from behind to spin or upend me, or someone else might insert his shoulder between my legs and hoist me up into the air, F. watching intently. Sometimes, when I was swooping about in the air, he would whistle mightily in different pitches as if he were a whole orchestra, with a melodic downslide as I descended. As long as I wasn't dropped too hard, I was relieved to be set back down again on the floor, but after a while I relished more the airborne sensation, the odd lightness of my body when it was ten feet up in the air. I liked the new way my body could be handled by someone, thrown about in space, spun, and molded. The same boy or a string of boys could perform all these feats of partnering; it hardly mattered. Everything they did to me, every move we made, was at F.'s command, controlled and orchestrated by him. They would lift or spin me in his stead, begin when he told them what to do, and release me at his nod. Clearly he preferred to stand at one side and watch, giving directions in his usual ironic manner; he would tease me with an insult while arranging the boy's hands around my waist or under my thigh.

What I most remember of my introduction to pas de deux is not how Ivan or Chico or anyone else partnered me; rather it is the intensity of F.'s watchfulness when someone else, some other ballet boy—it didn't matter who—took hold of me at his request, lifting me and setting me down with the choreography and rhythms F. determined. Although he had given me over to others to handle, F. remained my lodestar, the magnetic north of my compass, the man to whom I always looked and for whom I always danced, no matter whose hands were on me. No matter who partnered me, F., I knew, never took his eyes from me; it was his glance that held me even more tightly than Ivan's large hands.

Just before daily class one Monday, we Advanced students noticed a small piece of lined paper haphazardly taped to the studio door. Within seconds we all swarmed around it apprehensively, instinctively alert as dancers always are to the shifting currents of favoritism and power, like bees apprehending a threat to their hive. "Coppelia Audition," the paper said in a barely legible scrawl. "Sat., 10 A.M., Studio One. Girls: Black leotard, pink tights. Bring toe shoes. Boys: black tights, white T-shirt. Come warmed up & prepared to spend the day."

Martine and I stood shoulder to shoulder with our classmates, examining the notice over and over for its every nuance of meaning. We had never seen *Coppelia*, but we knew what it was: a lighthearted ballet about a buffoonish young man who mistakenly falls in love with a doll until he is united at the ballet's end with Swanhilda, his ever true love. Music by Delibes, some of which Mr. Shurbanov routinely played for class. Lots of parts for soloists and corps de ballet. "Is this audition for us, do you think?" I asked. "It better be," Martine retorted. I could feel her excitement, the tension and determination in her body as she nodded.

Just then F. walked over and surveyed our tight little group buzzing with anxiety and all of us jockeying for position in front of the notice to get a better look. Squinting and pointing with two fingers as if he were sighting along a gun, F. fixed Martine and then me in his imagined crosshairs. "You two," he said. "Get here early." Stretching out his arm to its full length, he pointed decisively to five more girls. "You. You. You. You. And you." Amanda. Jocelyn. Diane. Susu. Rosalie.

Martine and I exchanged a look: seven of us chosen to audition, but she and I already felt like soloists. Then with a big sweep of his arm and loud blasts of whistling as if he were directing traffic at a crowded intersection, F. waved us into class and to the barre. As we started our first position *pliés* I could hear muffled sniffling from the girl right behind me: Sharon—poor Sharon—had been left out of the audition list. By *battements fondus* and *ronds de jambe* the tears were streaming down Sharon's face, but neither I nor anyone else paid the slightest attention.

Early Saturday morning Martine and I met in the dressing room, pulled on our practice clothes—black leotard, pink tights—and began our stretches. "Come on," Martine urged. "We'll give each other a barre." Opening up two rickety folding chairs, we held on to their backs and began to stretch the tendons of our feet, pawing the slippery floor and pressing our feet against the linoleum in the atavistic, catlike motions dancers always perform to start their exercises. We put some spit on the soles of our shoes for traction, and then Martine called out a combination of steps for both of us. I followed, the two of us going back and forth in the traditional, unchanging routines of the barre, but my body felt cold and unmalleable, my mouth dry with apprehension of the unknown audition to follow. Meanwhile other girls were trooping in, droves and fleets of dancers in all sizes and shapes—*where did they all come from?* I wondered. They changed their clothes and grabbed all the other available chairs for their own barre exercises—Amanda, Jocelyn, Diane, Susu, Rosalie, and packs of girls we had never before seen, all of them dressed identically and soon busy with their own *frappés* and *grands battements.*

I'll never make it, I thought. *They're all much better than I am. Maybe Martine, but not me.* "Who *are* these girls?" I asked Martine in an undertone. "Have you ever seen any of them? Some of them are so old!"

She had seen a few, she said; she thought they were in F.'s professional class. The others?—must be from "around town." "By the way," she went on dryly, continuing her *grands battements en croix,* "yesterday I overheard F. telling Sonya, 'Let them audition. It will be good experience.'"

"Oh, God! That means we won't get in."

"Of course we will," Martine asserted definitively. "We're his pets. I think he meant Susu and the rest of them. So what?" She grabbed my leg and shoved it up over my head, pushing it with both hands from underneath until I was standing in an almost-split. It hurt but felt good; involuntarily I drew in a deep breath. "Now do me," Martine ordered.

Without having received any signal, all of us in our identical practice clothes surged toward the studio a few minutes before ten. Sonya, looking officious, roamed the room with a clipboard taking names and telephone numbers, while another woman pinned a large white card to the back of my leotard with a number written on it in black. "Twelve," Sonya noted on her clipboard when she got to me. "Name?"

Martine twirled around so that I could see her number—eight—and pronounced the two of us lucky. But I felt more bewildered in this crowd than lucky, my muscles shaky with stage fright despite my warm-ups. Suddenly I felt myself watched—and there was F., lurking in a corner at the far side of the room, his gaze fixed on me, his ever present cigarette in the side of his mouth. When he caught my eye he languidly removed the cigarette and almost imperceptibly nodded a greeting. *I'll be okay,* I thought with relief. *F. wants me to win this.* But just as quickly the relief vanished, and I wished that I could stand on the sidelines with F., smoking languidly as he did, remote and above it all. Why couldn't I just be "chosen" without having to audition? From inside the studio, I could hear the pianist playing chords and scales, and again I felt the cold shivers of stage fright.

Soon we were lined up by Sonya in numerical order and counted off one by one into the studio where we took our assigned places at the barre. A short pudgy man in a dark suit and tie entered the room at the head of a phalanx of what I took to be judges: F., still looking languid and taking one last drag on his cigarette before stabbing it out in an ash-tray by the door; a plump bright-eyed woman in stiletto heels and a turban; and another man, lanky and sallow with long sideburns and an untidy moustache. Then Sonya with her clipboard. The pudgy man carried a heavy walking stick that he banged ceremoniously on the floor. "First position, girls and boys," he barked out while the judges receded against the wall to watch us. He nodded to the pianist to begin.

Halfway through our first sequence, the man in charge again rapped on the floor with his stick to stop us and then started us off on something completely different. Such, I quickly learned, was the pattern of an audition: nothing finished, everything interrupted, so that the observers could get a quick glimpse of what we could do. Every now and again the pudgy man would confer with F. and the lanky man with the unkempt moustache; meaningful looks would be directed at one or the other of us and then Sonya would hurriedly write something on her clipboard. As I began to enjoy the stop-start rhythm of the audition, I unexpectedly caught F.'s eye. He winked at me, and then made a face in mock imitation of the pudgy man barking at us with his brusque, businesslike commands. Suddenly everyone but F. seemed so absurd—the little man with his self-important stick, now sweating with the exertions of our barre even more profusely than we were; the man with the handlebar moustache who seemed to be having trouble staying awake; all of us with our silly numbers pinned to our backs as if no one knew who we really were. I had to bite my lip to keep from laughing, and when I dared to look again at F. he winked at me a second time and gave me a surreptitious sign with his encircled fingers: victory.

After a quick barre, we took our places in the center for some cursory jumps and turns interrupted, as usual, by a sharp rap on the floor and a new set of directions. In the middle of a pirouette combination, the pudgy man banged again and then unexpectedly bowed to us. "Thank you," he said. "Girls can go. Boys please stay. Thank you, ladies." Another bow. We scooped up our dance cases from the under the barre and got out as quickly as we could. The boys were crashing around behind us in double *tours en l'air.* Spend the day? It was all over so quickly, and we hadn't even been asked to put on our pointe shoes. Out in the hallway over the water fountain, where we would be sure to see it, was another handwritten sign in the same scrawl. "You will be notified," it said. "Don't call us, we'll call you."

The cast list was posted at our next class. All the major roles would be taken by professional dancers, their names starred with asterisks as former students of F.'s, while current students from his school and elsewhere would become corps de ballet, performing the ballet's folk dances, its mazurka and czardas. When I saw that all seven of us had been listed for something or other, I realized immediately that the audition had actually occurred long before we entered that room, and F.'s tipping me off had made perfect sense. We seven were all corps de ballet, of course, I in the mazurka, Martine in the czardas. But, to my great surprise, I was listed as understudy for two additonal roles. The first was the solo called "Prayer" in Act 2. Then, along with Martine, I was understudy for one of Swanhilda's "friends," a role I knew nothing whatsoever about except that a "friend" was in all three acts, and therefore, I hoped, got to do a lot of dancing. In turn, one of the girls listed as a "friend" understudied Swanhilda. Rehearsals would start immediately.

Right away I was plunged into a schedule of constant rehearsing; there was something to do almost every evening after class and each day over the weekend. Because I was understudying two roles and had my own corps de ballet dancing to do, I was almost always on call, at least to observe and learn my solo parts even when I might not ever get the chance to dance them. The "friend" to whom I was assigned at the first rehearsal was an older dancer named Tina who had platinum hair and bold red lipstick; I disliked her immediately for looking so tarted-up instead of resembling the dark-haired, almond-eyed ballerina of my ideals. Martine was linked with a "friend" named

Natasha who at least had a Russian name. Tina and Natasha nodded to us coldly as if warning us to stay out of their way and then returned to their own conversations. "Should we slip nails into their toe shoes?" Martine whispered, her Slavic eyes narrowed. "Fix them a little cocktail?"

Of course I fell in love with "Prayer." With ballet as my religion, I could claim "Prayer" as the essence of every moment I dedicated to dance; I would have given anything to be able to perform the solo and not just mark it, shadow-dance it in the background. The choreography was perfect for me. Simple and undemanding, it was all quick *bourrées* (those hours stumbling at the barre!) and langorous *arabesques penchées*. Even better, "Prayer" was performed in a virginal white nightgown, the dancer all the while gazing rapturously upon a long-stemmed white lily held in pious, outstretched hands. Suffused with the religion of dance—its piety, self-abnegation, devotion—I imagined myself a young novice in a convent, for whom "Prayer" was the lyrical embodiment of my inner dedication and holiness. I learned the solo in a flash.

My chance arrived one afternoon when F.'s ancient mother, our revered Madame F. from St. Petersburg, had come on one of her heralded visits to the studio, where she observed our Advanced Class, mother and son identically beak-nosed and angular, both dragging nonchalantly on their cigarettes. When class was dismissed—after our *grandes révérences* and curtsies to an imaginary audience and then to F. and Madame F., and after the cursory applause that ends every class and continues as the dancers troop out the door—F. whistled to get my attention and told me to stay behind.

"Prayer," he ordered, handing me his cane as a prop for the long-stemmed lily and directing me to the back corner of the studio as if it were the far wings of a stage. "Madame wants to see you." I stationed myself in the imaginary wings, F. nodded to Mr. Shurbanov to begin, and I rose on pointe for my *bourrées*, devoutly holding F.'s cane in front of me, my hands reverentially clasped around it and my face tilted upward toward heaven. I was rapturous. Afterward Madame kissed the top of my head while F. looked on, beaming. I felt flushed, blessed.

But Swanhilda's "friend" was a different matter. Self-righteously—and unaware that in a professional ballet company even the corps de ballet roles are understudied—I considered understudying a "friend" beneath me. Understudying "Prayer" was one thing, but being a mere understudy for a role that five girls danced in a line, like Rockettes? Not for me, I decided. I resolutely refused to learn it.

When I look back now, still embarrassed at my decision, I can barely imagine how a young dancer, just out of her white-socked, baby-ballet days and the lowliest member of a new company, could have behaved with such naive arrogance. Every phase of my training had instilled in me compliance; every atom of my body yielded to the demands of the ballet master, to the discipline inherent in our search for artistic perfection. I should have learned the "friend's" part the first time I saw it danced, picked it up almost by osmosis, just as I learned everything else in class. Over and over dancers are required to reproduce choreographic patterns instantaneously, either by watching someone perform, or by hearing someone call out the steps, or—as I did with F.—by intently watching little flicks and jumps of the ballet master's hands, a "shorthand" understood like a code between initiates. Once a dancer "gets" the basic pattern, slotting it into kinetic memory, changes can be performed on it instantly—changes of direction or timing, reversing the order of steps and even reversing the steps themselves, so that a pirouette that is "inside" becomes "outside," and so on. While dancers are not known for their quick-wittedness, a dancer who sees something once—only once—can usually replicate it exactly. To a dancer if not to a real person, it is nothing to step in unrehearsed and perform a new role to perfection. So, since I was in rehearsal day after day, for me *not* to have learned the role of Swanhilda's friend took rigorous effort: I must have averted my eyes or turned my back each time the choreography was performed. I would have had to blind myself.

The dancers imported by F. for Swanhilda and her friends were a ravaged bunch anyway, not much fun to watch, and certainly not as inspiring as the dancers of my imagination or the ones whose photographs I pored over in books and ballet programs; they were older, rangier "girls," who had knocked around in various ballet companies apparently never getting very far. *Especially Tina,* I thought. They kept themselves separate from the younger dancers, smoking a lot and wisecracking to each other. I, on the other hand (or so I thought), was pure as a nun: I had my "Prayer," a steady *arabesque penchée,* a scrubbed complexion, and my own natural hair color—unexceptionable mouse brown, to be sure, but my own. There was little need to emulate a second-rate soloist who refused to acknowledge that I existed. *I* was going to be a great dancer.

But one day word went around that Tina had been in a car accident, a small one, nothing major, but she certainly was not going to appear for rehearsal that day. We all suspected that the "car accident" was a hoax or a hangover: Tina had probably just decided to take the day off. Rehearsals were often long, tedious affairs, and she undoubtedly had better things to do. Perhaps she was having her platinum hair touched up; perhaps she was having a fight with the boyfriend who picked her up after rehearsals and who was rumored to have occasionally blackened her eyes. Perhaps she had stayed out too late. In any case, if F. called a rehearsal of Act 1, I would have to step in as a "friend." I knew I hadn't learned much of Tina's role, but I didn't care.

F. must have had some doubts about Tina's commitment, too, because he started the rehearsal in a dark mood, morose and glowering. He pulled a wooden folding chair to the center of the ballet studio, against the mirrored wall, and sat tensely on the edge of it, facing us. "From the beginning," he ordered, rapping against the floor with his cane. Franz appeared from stage left, miming his love for Coppelia, unaware that she was merely a lifelike doll set up to entice him, and then Swanhilda entered with her pack of friends, including me.

At first the choreography was engaging, a lot of comical running about doing broad pantomime gestures. Being a friend was surprisingly more fun than I had thought and certainly livelier than dancing "Prayer." Soon, though, Swanhilda and her friends started their own dance, just the six of them. In a line with the others, I danced a few steps until my dance memory petered out. Glancing quickly at the five dancers around me, I recalled a few more steps, but within moments I was not at all able to keep going.

F. interrupted us. "Begin again, please," he instructed. We took our places, the pianist started, and this time I managed to remember a few more bars of choreography. But again I faded.

F. rapped with his cane. "Evan alone," he said nodding at me as if he hadn't had his eyes on me the whole time, observing me stumble and lag. He seemed weary, preoccupied, irritable, as if he just wanted to get this part of the dance over with and move on to something else, if only I would cooperate by doing the right steps. Swanhilda and her other four friends retreated to the barre at the back of the studio where the rest of the company was by now watching me nervously. The pianist began again, the same few bars, and again I danced the first few sequences of the variation—this time alone and in the center of the studio—until my mind went blank and I stopped dead.

Mr. Shurbanov optimistically played on at the piano for a few moments and then he, too, came to a halt. Silence. I stood still, in fourth position like a Degas dancer, my hands on my hips, waiting. I hadn't even danced enough to be out of breath.

F. rapped with his cane and nodded to the pianist. "Again," he said. I knew I would get no further in the choreography than the last time, it was hopeless, and I knew moreover that F. *also* knew it was hopeless: I clearly didn't know a thing, could *never* do this dance no matter how often F. made me stand in the center of the studio repeating over and over again the same paltry sequence of steps. He was clearly ordering me to dance "again" in order to humiliate me, to prove to everyone that I had stupidly not learned what I should have picked up in an instant. Obviously I didn't know a thing and would never be a dancer. I would never be Swanhilda's friend, nor would I ever get a shot again at "Prayer." I steeled myself for the humiliation, danced my few little steps, and stopped helplessly.

"Again!" F. commanded angrily, having demonstrated to everyone that I had no idea of the choreography. But he had evidently decided to torture me with his demand, to show me and everyone else in the room how inept I was—me, the young star, the pet, the favorite, who could learn anything in an instant but who now could do nothing but stand there dumbly. When the pianist started the same few bars of music, I didn't even bother to try again but just stood in the center of the studio, grim and immobile. "Again," F. repeated savagely. "You. From the top."

I didn't move.

F. rose out of his wooden chair with such force that it clattered to the floor behind him. Slowly he walked toward me. For every step he took toward me I involuntarily took a step backward until I had backed myself to the barre at the wall and could go no further. With F. advancing on me, I tried to disappear though the wall, but the barre just pressed into the small of my back, holding me there. Everyone else had moved aside.

F. glared at me, took aim, raised his cane. But he didn't hit me. Instead he smashed the cane against the barre with such force that I could feel the vibration in the wood where I was pressed against the barre. For a second I reeled; I thought he had struck me. Then he hurled his cane across the room. "Get out!" he shouted. "Rehearsal canceled! All over! Everyone out!"

Someone picked up his cane and gingerly handed it back to F. as he headed for the door like a cyclone, while all of us trooped out of the ballet studio behind him, stunned. Or, rather, I should say that everyone else fled en masse—girls and boys, the entire company—grumbling that no sooner had they gotten to rehearsal than they were sent home: What a wasted day. But I was not part of the pack. Everyone gave me a wide berth, as if I were suddenly quarantined. The girls in the dressing room glanced at me with what I interpreted as a look of mixed horror and fascination, glad they were not in trouble, wondering what my fate would be.

I wondered about it myself in some inchoate, almost drugged way. From experience we all knew that *something* had to happen: There would be an event, some significant repercussion for my arrogance, my lapse of responsibility. F. wasn't one to have a temper tantrum and then let it go at that, as if the mere display of fury were enough. In fact the outburst was unlike him, out of character, so I certainly expected that once his rage subsided, I would be the guilty focus of his more controlled and punctilious anger. I also knew I deserved it. It was just a matter of time.

So I fled to a far corner of the dressing room and curled up on a bench like a hunted animal, hugging my knees, making myself as small as possible, while everyone else hurriedly dressed and left. Soon I was alone in my dark corner, my mouth dry and my mind an utter blank. Not only could I not have danced *Coppelia* at that moment, I could not even have recited my name and address.

After a while—a long while, it seemed—one of the dancers approached me gingerly. F. wanted to see me, she reported. In his office. I didn't respond; a numbing amnesia had settled over me. The girl disappeared, evaporated into thin air as if she were disembodied. A few hours went by, it seemed, while I continued to hide: A darkness was setting over the face of the earth or at least over the girls' dressing room, and then another girl, or perhaps the same girl—faceless, indistinct—appeared in front of me and repeated the same message. Again I didn't respond, and the messenger disappeared. Nothing could move me; I was paralyzed. Much later someone else equally faceless appeared where I was entombed, and announced in what I thought was a brutally loud and abrasive voice, "F. says that if you don't get right up to his office, he's coming down here for you." I nodded.

I hadn't had the energy to change my clothes and was still in my leotard, but I slowly uncurled myself and headed uncertainly for the stairs. I walked up a step at a time, pausing every now and then to breathe and then, at the thought of F. coming down the stairs to fetch me himself, continuing my slow progress. Soon I was in the hallway to his secret room, and then at the door. The building was totally quiet; it felt to me as if everyone in the universe had gone home, except for me. And F., on the other side of his door.

I knocked, hoping that F. wouldn't hear me, that I could become a mere sliver of myself and then disappear into thin air. Instead I heard a quiet "Come in."

Slowly I opened the door, stepped in, expecting F. at the doorway, expecting him to fill the door entirely as if he were a menacing genie let out of a bottle and filling up the whole room.

Instead, F. was lying flat on his back on the couch, his knees up. Naturally, I had never before seen F. in any position but upright, striding around, marking things for us to dance, leaning nonchalantly on the barre. It seemed so odd, so vaguely terrifying, to look down on this man flat on his back, his knees up, when the last time I had seen him he had been standing not two feet from me, glowing with rage and hurling his cane like a thunderbolt.

With both hands he was fingering the ends of his leather cane, bending and flexing it, playing with it. He didn't look up or even move when I entered, but continued rhythmically to flex his cane. Now and again he would swish it sharply across his own legs, as if he were anticipating, practicing, what he would do to me. He didn't even give me a glance.

I closed the door behind me and stood there silently, waiting for F. to rise and confront me. There was silence, just the slight movement from F. as he bent his cane and then flicked it across his legs almost as if I weren't there. Now that I was enclosed in his room with him, I was mesmerized, beyond fear, hypnotized by the soft repeated switching of his cane. Watching him, I felt preternaturally alert, but it was also as if I were drinking anesthesia: Parts of my brain were flickering while other parts had entirely shut down. *Did it hurt?* I could hear him saying from some well of memory. *Do you want it again?* Finally F. broke the silence.

"Do you want to be a great dancer?" he asked.

I knew what he meant. It was a brutal question.

∾

If this were fiction, F. would have made love to me here. It's the right moment.

The older man examines the girl from where he is lying on the couch, and her body stiffens; she is expecting to be struck, knowing that she deserves it and will allow it. Her body is rigid, not with fear but with premonition and a kind of longing for whatever will happen to her. Instead of rising to punish her, however, he tells her to take off her practice clothes. "Get undressed," he says in a low voice, so quietly that she can hardly hear him. Confused, she does nothing at all for a moment until he repeats the request and then she begins to do as he says, sliding her arms out of the black stretch leotard and lowering it over her hips and buttocks, never taking her eyes off of the man lying there watching intently. She hardly leans over to step out of the leotard because she doesn't want to bend down or look away even for a second; she doesn't want anything to happen that she can't see and protect herself against, so she raises each leg, pulling the leotard down. Then she folds it carefully, as if she were packing it back into her dance case, but not knowing what else to do and not wanting to turn around, she just holds the leotard awkwardly in her hand. "Your tights," he says, and now she has to drop her leotard to the floor to use both hands while she slips out of her ballet shoes and rolls her tights down from her waist, pulling them with some difficulty from her feet. She folds the tights neatly and drops them on top of her leotard. Without being told, she removes her training bra and lets that, too, drop to the floor. It takes so few movements for her to remove all of her clothes. Now she is naked, barefoot, a little feral because she is trapped. She has never been naked in front of a man before.

He stands up slowly, the cane still in his right hand. He raises his left to touch her hair, but she flinches, and then because she has flinched, he drops his cane; she hears it clatter against the floor. With both hands he cups her face for a moment, and then gently but methodically loosens her dancer's bun, taking out hairpin after hairpin, and then the elastic holding her ponytail, until all her hair is released and she shakes it loose around her shoulders. Now he takes her firmly around the waist as if he were about to lift her up into the air but instead presses her waist until she bends her knees in a funny bow and sits down on his couch, keeping her back straight because that is what dancers do. Quickly, in one movement, he lifts her legs and lowers her body until she is lying down where he himself was just a few moments ago, on her back as he was, but naked, and now he sits next to her.

For a moment he hesitates. Tentatively, as if he had not touched her all over her body wherever he wanted to every day for the past two years, he strokes her with his hand: her ribcage, her stomach. He traces her collarbone with his fingertip, cups her hips, her breasts, gently touches the soft flesh on the inside of her thigh where he had once hit her. She winces then, with memory, even though now he isn't hurting her at all.

Soon, he will easily push her legs apart—easily, because she is used to having the parts of her body moved and stretched by him. She is used to the way he arranges her legs; he has done it every day in class. So you couldn't say that she is afraid of him; what she feels isn't fear. On the contrary, she gives in to him, allows her body to be pliable to his will as if all along she were expecting him to expose and arrange her this way, as if she were a part of a tableau he is choreographing. Even though she is mute— and he, too, is silent, tense—she moves wherever his touch directs her as if there is a faint thread of music in the background, or a voice calling out the counts. *And one . . . and two . . . and three . . . and four . . .* She never looks away from his face, never closes her eyes, not even for a second. She opens her legs.

The scene has no ending.

As far as I know, what I describe here never happened, much as I would like now to recall the scene this way; I like writing this lovemaking as if it were true. But F. didn't make love to me. He didn't hit me.

Nor did he even touch me. He didn't even get up from his couch. Did I want to be a great dancer? I suppose I nodded. But even more than becoming a great dancer, I wanted something to happen, almost anything, to release me from standing near this supine man, watching him bend his leather cane and hit himself with it almost absentmindedly, as if he were in a trance. I felt like a voyeur.

Try as I might, I cannot remember what happened after F. asked me his question. My memory closes like a trap over the sight of F. lying on his couch, switching himself—*ping!*—instead of striking me, making me feel his anger. Perhaps he lay there forever, flexing his cane with his fingertips, and I stood next to him, forever waiting for something to happen. Perhaps neither of us ever moved. Because this lovemaking scene is fantasy, and therefore I cannot "remember" that anything like it ever happened, and in fact all I can truly remember is darkness, emptiness, blankness, I know that now, right now in these words that give me so much pleasure, I am making up the ending to this story because I so badly wanted some confrontation, some release. It could have been sex, it could have been punishment, we could both have turned into pillars of salt or pillars of smoke in some cataclysmic act of transformation—I would not have known the difference, so long as there was a final, fitting act to bring this humiliating drama to a halt.

But there was none. The next thing I know for sure, the next moment securely fixed in a clear trajectory of memory, is that I am in the hallway heading back to the dressing room, walking away from F. as somnambulantly as I had walked toward him.

I should have been relieved but I wasn't, not at all. I felt throttled, disappointed, let down. Even deceived. Something in me had been thwarted, some impulse short-circuited. Inwardly, silently, I screamed and cried, more than I ever would have had F. actually struck me again and again. I bit my tongue, I bit my own hand, I wanted something so badly. I wanted some sensation so nameless, so hidden, that I had no idea what to call it, no idea if what I was crying for even existed. Full of thwarted desire, I wanted to throw myself against the walls.

He *should* have made love to me; I see that now. He should at least have hit me. If he had chosen to come toward me, if he had caressed me or simply ordered me to take off my practice clothes and then taken me with no explanation or affection, as if it were his painful but necessary duty, I would have surrendered to him. Completely, without question. All I really know is that I left F.'s office at some signal from him, somehow—I don't know how—but nothing had happened. Nothing I can remember. Instead, F. is forever pinned in my memory lying flat on his back whipping himself hard enough to hurt.

*   *   *

What did F. teach me? That the spectrum of sex is very wide. And that it doesn't necessarily include ordinary intercourse. When a little girl stands beside a man, rigid with fear but wishing to surrender to him because she willfully adores him, always has and always will, and they are locked together with bolts of steel in a secret room that no one else enters and where anything can happen, and when you, in fact, are that little girl, then you have already learned that one human being can possess another with barely a touch exchanged. What I knew was that even standing stock-still I brimmed over with expectation—no, not mere expectation, but longing so intense that every fiber of my body yearned for attention, for crisis, for the sharp, still point of pain or pleasure.

Part 3

~ *Solo*

After F. released me from his secret room, leaving with me the indelible vision of a man turning his rage (no: his desire) back upon himself, I hastily numbed myself to what had happened in that dark empty building with just the two of us there late in the day. For years I tried to forget everything that happened after F. hurled his cane across the studio and threw everyone out of rehearsal—I wanted to forget, I wanted amnesia, as if I could clamp a cone of ether over my face and black out.

But, instead of forgetting, for years I replayed the scenes in memory, looking for an ending to the story that moved from rehearsal to dressing room to hallway, and then to the moment I finally gathered the courage to open F.'s door to confront whatever awaited me inside.

F.'s threat—the immense, bitter threat of withheld desire and the thrill of danger—such a threat had become for me under F.'s tutelage the very seal of sexuality. I could see on the man's side a holding back to assess brutality and measure it with an eye keen to possibility; on my side I knew my desire to carry on these dangerous meetings in F.'s secret room, our whipsaw encounters inseparable from our shared vision of artistic bravura. Such was the gavotte we danced, courteous and almost savage, choreography not for the stage but for the clandestine room where, hidden away, I would have risked anything. F. had already taken me far from the playful courtship of boys like Danny, boys my own age whose erotic ambitions centered around a sweet little bout of communal homework. Not only was I not interested in math problems, but a romance based on tentative kisses paled next to the sweeps of tenderness and shafts of brutality I knew I could elicit from F.

Sometimes I even want to feel it again, the threat of that corrosive sting. The possibility is alluring, a thrill. Not because I want to get hurt or desire pain but because the ritual evokes for me the confusing, heady power of ambition and love.

With F.'s question echoing in my mind, and the rhythmic counterpoint of his cane flicking across his own legs, I went to the next rehearsal of *Coppelia* with a fervently anxious resolution: I would learn *all* the parts, from Swanhilda on down to the lowliest sequence for the corps de ballet. I promised myself that I would watch everything avidly, even the choreography for Franz and old Dr. Coppelius, just in case I might be required to step in again. For the time being, the last thing I wanted was a repeat performance in F.'s darkened room, waiting—even wildly longing—for F. to take some brutal action against me, willing a composure that I didn't feel and that would have crumbled in a second.

At rehearsal we all routinely took our places for a full run-through of the ballet as if nothing had happened with F. and we had been rehearsing smoothly for weeks. Knowing that I had been responsible for the previous disaster made me wary and self-conscious. But it turned out that not only I but the other dancers as well were practicing amnesia. In fact, dancers disregard reality all the time: "The show must go on," they say heedlessly. If someone suffers an accident in rehearsal or on stage, dancers will cover over the rift and continue as if nothing has happened, much as water instantaneously flows over a fissure in a streambed where a stone has been removed. A dancer can sprain an ankle or wrench a back or pull a tendon in performance and barely anyone will notice—certainly not the audience and sometimes not even all the other dancers until they get back into the wings and someone is writhing in pain with a doctor hovering and calling for ice. One is cold-blooded, disregarding, insistent that the performance continue, even if it is one's own leg that is broken. So no one paid attention to me, even when I moved around in back of the soloists learning and marking their steps. F. whistled, called for repeats, directed traffic, acted as if I didn't exist.

But something of F.'s simmering anger at me, at Tina, at the whole lot of us, seemed to hang over our rehearsals, sullying the air like continually discordant music. There were constant small explosions of tension between F. and packs of strangers milling about, new people none of us had ever seen before and who would watch us critically for a while and then stalk out of the studio followed by F. who had stopped Mr. Shurbanov's piano playing with an abrupt wave of his hand. One of these irritating phantoms was the man with the unkempt moustache and droopy sideburns whom I remembered from our audition. He turned out to be a Mr. Sergeyev, a lumbering Russian choreographer and ballet master even more ancient to our eyes than was F. Mr. Sergeyev always looked sallow to me, and half asleep, as if our dancing had awakened him from heavy slumber. He would watch us despondently, his eyes half closed, and then erupt in a torrent of Russian that he and F. would continue out in the hall, where they were almost—but not quite—out of earshot. We had to wait patiently during these interruptions, either going back to the barre for more warm-ups, lying on the floor to do stretches, darning our shoes, or sometimes even getting out a deck of cards. The older girls and boys would light their cigarettes and puff smoke out the window until F. returned.

"Places," F. would order abruptly, snapping his fingers and pointing at Swanhilda as if the rehearsal had been proceeding smoothly all day. "From where you come in. The door opens, move out quickly, you're excited"—F.'s tone was businesslike—"farther out, farther out. The door has to close behind you, yes? Yes. Look right, look left: Maybe Franz is around, yes?—*Now* go! And one . . ."

Every time the door opened onstage and the girl was framed in the doorway, ready to rush out, I felt a surge of some sensation I can only call heat, some mixture of dread and exaltation overtaking my body as if it were a rash. Perhaps it was just stage fright, but I felt as if I were opening the door to F.'s secret room, venturing into sudden dangers and hidden enticements. For Swanhilda just as for me, a door opens, a girl dances through it, and her life is changed forever.

When I saw again and again in rehearsal the opening of Swanhilda's cottage door, I remembered as well the same scene in the long-ago performance of *Giselle* my parents had taken me to as my introduction to classical ballet. Even as Swanhilda and Franz romped through this silliest of all ballets, the dark gestures of *Giselle* remained imprinted in the synapses of my memory: Giselle shyly, lightheartedly entering the stage to dance her innocent, doomed love with Albrecht; Giselle plucking the petals of a daisy to pantomime he-loves-me, he-loves-me-not; Giselle raising the back of her hand to her forehead, head thrown back, when she felt faint, when she foretold her death. *Oh, Mother, leave me alone! I am a young girl in love. I will dance anyway, even if I die!*

As in my childhood, when I had pantomimed Giselle's mad scene in the aisle of the theater, so now I imagined myself as Swanhilda, and began learning her choreography as if someday I would dance it myself. I skittered downstage with her, crouched and knocked my knees together in comic terror, loved the acting, the mime, the ballet kind of falling in love, in which the boy clasps both hands to his heart and yearns and the girl circles her face with her fingertips, knowing she is radiantly lit with love.

But F., apparently, had had enough of us, or so it seemed to me when we villagers were divided from the rest of the cast and began to practice at different times or in a separate studio. I was terribly disappointed and complained to Martine that it felt as if we were just an ordinary ballet school preparing for our annual recital—not that I had ever been in one. But I felt diminished, demoted back into the corps de ballet, as if separate rehearsal space were another humiliating consequence of my failure to learn the ballet.

Not only were we corps de ballet girls separated from the soloists, but it turned out that Sonya rather than F. was now in charge of us; she was the ballet mistress who "took" our rehearsals of the crowded czardas and mazurka. *F. doesn't care about me,* I thought. *He has betrayed me.* Or sometimes I thought, *I have betrayed him, and that's why he's given us over to Sonya.* When I hazarded these opinions to Martine, trying to sound casual about F.'s casting all of us into the exile of rehearsal with Sonya, she just raised her eyebrows. "Ballet politics," she said cryptically. "Nothing to do with us." And then she zeroed in on what was really haunting me. "Don't worry, you're still teacher's pet." But Martine was as dissatisfied with Sonya as I was. Nor did Sonya herself seem especially happy about her new duties, joylessly making us repeat our dances again and again until we inwardly groaned each time we heard the opening bars of our music. Sonya, despite her grim determination to fill our bloodstream with beats of czardas and mazurka, never seemed happy with our progress and, as rehearsals wore on, became more and more tense and irritable. We could often hear her arguing with F. out in the hallway as we took a break; she would return to us with her dark eyes flashing and a determined look on her face. "Once more," she would say sternly waving us to our places. "*Dee—da da da—dum dum dum—*girls—get ready. . . ."

* * *

Although F.'s rehearsals were now closed to me (and, obviously, to the rest of the corps de ballet as well, although I didn't see it that way), we still took class every afternoon with F., and now, even more than before, I did whatever I could to make myself the perfect little dancer, the apple of her teacher's eye. If anything, my desire for *his* desire had sharpened. More than ever I wanted to be—still *deserved* to be, I thought—the center of his attention.

Now that I was fourteen and not the unformed child who first entered F.'s class, now that I was almost a dancer and beginning to perform for real, I was increasingly aware of how to orchestrate attention, how to command an audience, even an audience of one. I *knew* I had changed: No longer was my mother setting out on my bed those rows of long-sleeved, full-skirted cotton dresses with their Peter Pan collars and sashes or cinch belts. Now she was bringing home for me matched sweater sets in pastels with pearly buttons, knife-pleated wool skirts (still plaids), even a red wool blazer that is still in my closet and that I could wear even today. She still saw to it that I wore a slip under my skirt, but she had added stockings, pumps, and the occasional pair of soft doeskin gloves. And now, instead of sewing my party dresses out of taffeta, she bought for me a black velvet skirt and a

beaded black satin top with a square neck and cap-
sleeves that I adored.

But I had changed inwardly, too, perhaps because I
was just simply older (even if only by two years), but
also because all along I had been learning F.'s lessons.
Not only lessons in ballet technique but also his
lessons in attention and withdrawal, in keeping the
complexities of power lodged on your side. Some
years earlier I had had an encounter with an older man
that at first had shocked me but that had also illumi-
nated for me a certain kind of power that I had not
known I possessed. When I feared that F. was disregarding me, that his attention (or love, or fury) had
moved elsewhere, I had already begun to understand
that young girls are not always fragile as a dewdrop on
a summer's day.

The encounter had happened just about the time I
had first entered F.'s class. My family had taken all of
us on a short vacation to the beach, the last vacation I
would take with them for years. I knew when my parents planned the vacation—and my parents probably
knew it, too—that those two short weeks would be
the last time for a long while that I would be free to
get away from the ballet world for any semblance of
family life. We stayed in a small cottage near the
beach—myself, my parents, a brother and sisters—in
the kind of beach house that's equipped for the transient life of vacationers wanting sun and sand, open

space, and not much privacy. Another family accompanied us, none of whom I had met before.

One late morning my family went to the beach, leaving me at home to start lunch, a pizza to prepare from a packaged mix. I was not in the habit of playing the family's Cinderella—in fact, I had barely done anything with my family since joining F.'s class—and I did enjoy the beach, but I stayed behind to do my ballet exercises, to practice on the linoleum floor using the kitchen counter for a barre. Trying not to lose my flexibility, I seized the chance to get all the kitchen space to myself even at the cost of preparing the lunch. Later I would join everyone at the beach; I had my bathing suit on.

I had rolled out the pizza dough into a circle and was spreading tomato sauce around when the door opened and Dr. Lyman entered. "Hello," I said, barely looking up and glad that no one had caught me with one leg up on the kitchen counter, stretching. He asked where my family was and I told him: At the beach. What was I doing? Making pizza. Oh. There was an embarrassed silence. I thought possibly I was supposed to entertain this man, make polite conversation, because, after all, he was an adult and a friend of my parents, but I had nothing to say. The doctor broke the silence. Suppose he took a look at the wounded rabbit we kids had found the day before, he suggested, the creature we were nursing back to health in a shoebox filled with grass. That seemed to me a good idea; after all, he was a doctor. I took him into the bedroom and bent over the little rabbit huddling in his box, the doctor right behind me, solicitous and caring. As I leaned over, he suddenly cupped his hands around my buttocks, both hands; and then he grasped my waist and breasts and pulled me around, pressing me to his chest as if he were about to kiss me. His hands seemed to tug and press all over me, everywhere. The hair on his chest felt warm and damp; it revolted me. As hard as I could I pushed him away, and with no inhibition about fighting with an adult, I slammed his shoulders with my fists. The doctor released me immediately without more struggle and stepped back, breathing hard and staring at me. He looked flushed and excited, and then a second later confused and miserable. "I'm sorry," he said hoarsely.

Then I didn't know what to do. I became exquisitely self-conscious, aware of my nipples and my buttocks under the thin nylon of my bathing suit, of my ribs where his hands had been pulling me toward him, of the nakedness of my legs, of my bare feet. But still, I felt I had to be polite, especially because I had already insulted him by struggling and hitting him—this kind, solicitous doctor, a friend of my parents. Dr. Lyman didn't seem to know what to do either. So I muttered something about having to make pizza and stumbled back into the kitchen, the doctor following me. He didn't try to touch me again, but he didn't take his eyes off me either; he seemed very worried. Once or twice he tried to say something—I think he even offered to help—but I wasn't about to encourage him, and finally he gave up and just watched me miserably as I took a spatula and finished spreading tomato sauce on the dough. I reached for the mozzarella topping, all preshredded, which came in a cellophane bag with a perforated edge. As I began to open it, my hands—as if they no longer belonged to me—began to behave in a peculiar quivering fashion, then suddenly shaking so violently that in one motion I ripped open the cellophane bag and involuntarily flung cheese in every direction all over the kitchen. Shredded mozzarella was everywhere, and I couldn't stop trembling. Overcome with fury, I started to yell. "Get out!" I yelled at the doctor. "Just get the hell out!"

"Mother!" I sobbed when she returned to see what was taking me so long. "Dr. Lyman attacked me." I was still shaking. Appalled and angry, my mother tucked me into bed with a tranquilizer, hot tea, and blankets, even though it was in the middle of the afternoon in the heat of summer. I was an invalid, violated by a trusted family friend, a father of young children, a pediatrician, of all things. For the rest of the afternoon, while presumably my mother alerted my father and the two of them confronted the doctor, I drifted in and out of a sweet drowsy amnesia.

Some days later I was on the beach with my parents huddled protectively around me. The doctor was there, too, sitting in a folding chair under an umbrella, his belly bulging over the same swimming trunks he had worn in my kitchen and his hairy legs stretched out in the sand. He kept his distance, didn't look up. I went into the water for a swim, and when I came back I noticed—or felt—that the man was staring at me again. It was clear from the expression on his face that he was still yearning to touch me despite the embarrassment he had occasioned, that given half a chance he would dissolve with hunger for me as he had in the kitchen; he couldn't help it. I definitely noticed it. I even flirted with him a little, dropping my towel, flashing him a knowing look, but as soon as he caught me looking at him he ignored me. I suddenly realized that in the kitchen he had revealed something about himself that he would never want anyone else to know—that he was driven, beyond control, sick with longing for a little girl. In the kitchen I had been confused, taken aback, shaken. But days later, in public and protected by my parents, I felt only fury and an unexpected surge of power: I wanted to torture him. I suddenly felt my sexuality as a kind of weapon; I knew I could aim it at him and make him flinch.

Sitting down on a towel I began to dry myself off, ostentatiously stretching my arms and legs, rubbing my towel over my body, knowing that the doctor was watching me, full of desire for me and afraid to show it. I patted myself and stretched, rubbed myself some more, and when I was finished drying off I put on a pair of white, heart-shaped sunglasses, like the ones Sue Lyon wore in *Lolita*, cocking my head in Dr. Lyman's direction as if to say, Now *how do you like me, practically naked, my eyes covered with hearts?* My mother finally noticed and got irritated. "Cover yourself up," she told me, handing me a terry beach robe. "Once is enough." Then I quickly became mutely obedient; I didn't mind listening to my mother as if I were still a child.

With that encounter reverberating in my memory, I began to explore a certain leeway in my (now somewhat desperate) relationship to F., as if a tight elastic band could, with effort, be stretched just a fraction more. I already knew—as every dancer does—that striving for perfection, even almost reaching it, will most often bring just a nod of approval from the ballet master, certainly not the exuberant praise one finds in real life for acts that little merit it. "Oh, fabulous!" real people blurt out constantly. "That's great!"—meaningless hyperbole to a dancer. For a dancer, as one's technical skills increase, praise is harder and harder to come by; a pleased nod by someone who knows what to watch for can be as satisfying as an accolade. But when a dancer does less than what is asked—or performs something poorly, or simply gets it wrong—

then the ballet master is there immediately at one's side, all condescension and commands. (*Sorry, my fault.*) In Advanced Class, where every tilt of the chin and flutter of an eyelash was determined by "the choreography," I always knew that if I deviated by a fraction, I was guaranteed F.'s attention. In the end, he could do as he wished with me—hurl insults at me, strike me whenever and however he chose—but I could, by merely being thirteen or fourteen and unformed, sometimes unsteady, capricious, playful, entice F. and keep him at my side. The balance of power—perhaps not so much a balance but more an unequal lurching back and forth—came from my growing knowledge that I could captivate him, that the ratios of power and desire could work to my advantage as well.

I knew that with F. I had to be audacious; I had to be willing to take risks, unlike Astrid who had become quiescent and would surely never become a great dancer. Astrid was too docile, and F. ignored her. Once she had returned from her failed escape to New York City, F. seemed to take her for granted, to know that she had no recourse but to stay with him, getting older and compliantly doing his bidding. He paid no attention to her except to wave her off on errands fetching cigarettes or coffee, asking her to bring him a folder from his desk drawer or to telephone the electrician when the power went off in the studio or to track down Mr. Shurbanov when he was late, all of which she performed with her usual sweetness. Much as I loved Astrid as big sister and confidante, I saw that she had *no personality* and would be stuck forever buying coffee and teaching Beginners Class.

So the method I chose to captivate F.—the only one I could have used, really—was not to towel off in front of him (he had seen a million dancers do that and couldn't have cared less) but to enhance my technique and then throw it to the winds. To be daring, whatever the consequence, to take risks, Russian-style or my style. To tease, to flaunt, to make demands. To dance like a whirlwind, to be willing to fail. Definitely to have *too much personality*.

From my first days in Advanced Class I had seen that F. always pushed us farther than we thought we could go; he made us stretch more, reach farther, kick higher, almost without regard for the restraints of technique. Certainly his demand for *more*, for a kind of bravura dancing, was at odds with the classical ideal of restraint and control, but with F. it sometimes seemed that *control*, the dancer's ideal that she can achieve supreme mastery over her body, such control could be heightened almost to its dissolution, as when a dancer balances on pointe for so long that she finally loses her balance and collapses (balletically, of course). It seemed that F. wanted me to go almost *out* of control, or, better, to deliver my body over to *his* control.

When I did an arabesque, he always wanted it higher; when I did *grands battements*, he wanted them more forceful, to the ceiling; when all of us as a class did something even so simple as *entrechats*, he wanted them to slice vertically through the air. And with a *grand jeté* he wanted us to soar into space and then, like Nijinski, to stay there. "Stay at the top," he would say, and that would mean: Go up as high as you can and then for a few seconds, for a lifetime, remain there, legs wide open in a split, poised in the air. He wanted force, speed, elevation. With a simple shrug of his shoulders and a dismissive, taunting look in his eye, he would make us hungry and daring. He would make us want to eat space.

Once Martine and I were assigned the same corps de ballet roles in *Coppelia* and understudied the same solo parts, we overtly competed with each other even though we were best friends, each of us trying to outdo the other in technique and bravura, in feats of daring or elevation or extension. If one of us could balance on pointe in arabesque a shade longer than the other and even longer than the music demanded, if we could spin so fast in *chainé* turns that our arms were a blur and we finally spun out of control, so much the better. Martine and I would go for broke.

But she was just enough older and stronger to be more skilled than I. In particular, I worried that I would never turn and spin as easily or forcefully as

Martine—all those pirouettes, *chaîné* turns, and *fouettés* that dancers practice daily from the very beginning of their training, whipping their heads around to "spot" an imaginary focal point in order to keep from getting dizzy. At the beginning of ballet training, though, as always one starts with the most minute aspect of technique: first, a quarter turn; then, a half turn, and so on, until a single pirouette can be executed perfectly. Yet especially in my first year with F., I often could not perform even a single turn with unerring accuracy; it was a hit-or-miss affair no matter how hard I concentrated and practiced. The prospect of performing the thirty-two *fouettés* required of Odile, the Black Swan, in the Act 3 pas de deux from *Swan Lake* terrified me, even though ballet girls routinely knock off thirty-two and even sixty-four *fouettés* as a whirling finale to every class. Martine could toss off any number of turns at breakneck speed, her head whipping around so fast that her hairpins would loosen and fly out in all directions, releasing a long mane of brown hair that swirled around with her while she continued, unconcerned.

So one day in class we were practicing the pirouettes I feared, in a simple combination calling for a series of single turns that just about anyone could do. I must have been falling all over myself, anxiously trying too hard, unable to rotate cleanly, with precision. F. was watching me as I floundered, chortling mirthlessly at first and then and calling out every insult he could think of. "Don't travel! Don't travel!" he would warn me just as I was getting started on my turns, to remind me—as if I needed it—to stay anchored in one place, not to allow my supporting foot to move across the floor by even a fraction of an inch. "Clumsy. Terrible," he taunted me when I helplessly "traveled." I tried again, spinning to a litany of shouted insults: "Worse!" F. was calling out. "Are you drunk?" "What are you doing with your arms? Don't pull them in like that—you look like a corpse!"

The dancer's code requires reacting with humble modesty no matter how insultingly one is treated, but I was working as hard as I could and beginning to get fed up. "Imbecile!" F. taunted me. Suddenly I became infuriated, livid. Anger and outrage nailed me to the floor as if my body were a steel rod; my rage fueled my turns. Instead of turning once I sailed through twice; instead of twice, three times, ending with a grand finale of four revolutions, perfectly executed. These pirouettes weren't improving, not "coming" as dancers say; they were whirling and blazing me around, they were *here*. I finished triumphantly, my arms flung out. Martine even applauded, best friend that she was. *Sensational!* I thought.

I casually ambled back to the barre and leaned against it, breathless and pleased with myself for turning into a dervish but finishing right on the music, not a nanosecond over. I faced F., half expecting him to compliment me but knowing that he might not, aware that my burst of turns might have exceeded by a wide margin the strict, precise demands of his choreography. I wanted the reward, but I was also daring him to confront me, to react to my evident victory.

F. slowly stood up, with that ironic, menacing look I recognized as a prelude to punishment. He grasped his cane and walked slowly toward me. I didn't budge or flinch—I didn't care, I had won that battle. He stopped directly in front of me, within hitting distance, and, truthfully, I would have stood there and taken it, no matter what; nothing could have damaged or hurt me, he could have whipped me to shreds and it wouldn't have made a difference. I knew I had won.

But instead of hitting me, he said one word under his breath: "Out." I had never been tossed out of class before, but I obeyed, naturally, taking my little terry-cloth towel from the barre, scooping up my dance case from underneath the barre, and slinging it nonchalantly over my shoulder. No one else moved; the other girls waited silently, almost somnolently, as I gathered up my stuff. F. didn't say a word either, but kept his eyes on me. "Next time don't change the choreography," he said to my retreating back as I sauntered out. *I will if I want to,* I thought, not deigning to look back. *You bet your sweet life.*

Even though I had been unexpectedly and embarrassingly thrown out of class and would have no more practice that day (what would I do with all that free *time*?), still I was proud of myself, pleased, and not a little triumphant. I had caught up with Martine— finally!—and surpassed myself in a way I never would have predicted. Whatever F. did to me, I didn't care: My fury had whirled me around in a perfect quadruple pirouette. Because my rage had propelled and stabilized me, the body—my own body—had accomplished something it had never before been capable of. F.'s parting sally about the choreography seemed weakly superfluous when I had so clearly won the contest between us. I even believed that F. in his parting shot was actually congratulating me.

The next afternoon, after I had been allowed back in class, F. beckoned me into his secret room. *It's because of the pirouettes,* I thought, *I'm in for it,* and my head began to whirl as dizzily as if I were spinning around again. But, no, F. apparently wanted to enjoy a companionable drink. After pouring my ginger ale, he raised his tumbler of vodka in my direction as if he were making a toast.

"You are just like Beriosova," F. said, downing the clear liquid in one shot. He meant Svetlana Beriosova, a favorite ballerina of mine, an exotically stylish Russian dancer at the Royal Ballet whose photographs in the Royal catalog I had pored over and tried to imitate. She was a mix of "Russian" bravura and icy British control, shining in a demure British setting and standing out from the placid, porcelain British dancers whom I had learned from F. to disregard. Comparing me to Beriosova was so unexpected, so extravagant a compliment that I could feel myself blushing with pleasure. So it *was* my flourish of pirouettes, my steely control, my bravura finish! He *did* adore me after all—because I was going to become a great dancer, even though I had failed as an understudy.

But I was still slightly uneasy. After all, my last encounter with him in this room had been to view him, sickeningly supine, using his cane on himself instead of (as we both seemed to want) using it to tear me apart. And wasn't I still showing off? Hadn't I learned anything? Cautiously I thanked F. and confided in him that I had once watched from the wings while Beriosova danced *Petrouchka*, devouring every step and nuance. F. interrupted me dourly. "All emotion. No technique. Can barely get through class."

Then it was my turn to be caustic. "If I have no technique," I said angrily, "it's your fault."

F. looked at me quizzically. Then he poured himself a second shot of vodka, raised his glass to me again, and quickly emptied it. Exhibiting *too much personality*, I saw, might not be as simple as I had thought. I might get myself thrown out of class again—even with Martine applauding me—but I might also have to answer to F. later, keeping myself on guard in a way that hadn't happened before; I might have to riposte with him as if we were peers and not a revered ballet master with his favorite student. I had loved that sensation of spinning around with angry energy, and loved, afterward, knowing that F. was pretty much helpless to do anything to me because, in fact, I was *good!*—no, not quite good, but getting better all the time, and maybe on the path to becoming a great dancer after all. But I wasn't quite sure how to react to F.'s bemusement in the secret room, so when he raised his second glass to me in another toast, I quickly polished off my ginger ale, stood up and thanked him politely, and waited for him to escort me to the door. Not saying a word and still looking bemused, F. gave me a quick pat on the cheek as I left.

But he had seen what I could do—spin brilliantly, even though my great whirling triumph in pirouettes had been an accident fueled by desperation and rage. As if I had given him the idea, F. soon afterward in class introduced us to a new way of increasing the speed of our turns. We were lining up to do endless *chainé* turns from one end of the studio to the other and back again when F. produced a hairbrush from his pocket and, one by one, hit the backs of our hands with the bristles. If we turned fast enough, our hands would be bloodied by centrifugal force. "Old Russian method," F. said cheerfully. It hurt a little, but more than the sharp pain I remember how difficult it was to force even a drop or two of blood to the surface of my hands and how pleased I was when I finally whirled fast enough to redden them. Not only did we not demur when instructed to hold out our hands, but we turned so fast that drops of blood sprayed out in all directions.

In truth, we all turned faster.

But, as in the pirouettes, where I turned and turned and could barely bring myself to stop, now more than ever I wanted to whirl toward F., forcing him to open his arms and catch me as if I were hurling myself at him through space in a *bolshoi* lift and he would have to be there, my partner, steady and dependable. But even while I wished to be the grand ballerina—commanding my imaginary stage and saying, "Begin again, Maestro"—I wanted also to be the young girl whom F. had originally singled out as his chosen one, the young dancer vulnerable to his power, willing to surrender herself to his authority and his vision of her. If he were the great ballet master, the legendary F., I would be the gifted pupil and submit to him, however he wished. I desired nothing more than to return to my earlier, sweeter days of submission, but I also sensed that I was beginning to outgrow my unalloyed reverence: I was growing up, changing, inevitably and almost against my will.

I became desperate to smoke, for example. On one level it seemed simple to me, and necessary. All dancers smoked cigarettes; it was axiomatic. The older dancers smoked like chimneys in the dressing rooms and in the vestibule outside the studios, poking their cigarettes out as they filed into class. Even Martine merrily lit up an occasional cigarette, smoking half of it and leaving a bright red lipstick smudge on its butt before she stubbed it out. All the teachers smoked; even Mr. Shurbanov smoked as he played the piano for our classes, pounding out the Czerny and the Chopin, an ashtray placed at the end of the keyboard. And of course F. himself was a chain-smoker, never seen even once in class without a cigarette stub burning down to his fingers while he stalked the class, nonchalantly ignoring how close he came to going up in flames. When he used both hands to mold our bodies he held his cigarette loosely in the corner of his mouth, a column of ash accumulating at its tip but never quite dropping to the floor. One of my most persistent memories is of F. looking at me sideways, eyes narrowed, head slightly cocked, a cigarette held in the slight ironic smile curling his mouth. No doubt I returned his ironic smile with a wisp of an ironic smile of my own, as if to say to F., *Whatever you're thinking—go ahead, just try it.*

"Please teach me," I begged Chico. We were all lounging around in the ballet lobby, talking, gossiping, and stretching in splits and contortions on the floor or against a wall for lack of anything better to do while we waited for class.

Chico lit a cigarette for me from his own and placed it in my mouth. I didn't understand yet about inhaling—and certainly not yet about dragging on a cigarette the way the older girls did—but I knew that the slender cylinder felt wonderful between my lips, especially since Chico had lit it for me. I puffed on it a few times and gave it back, not knowing what else to do with it, but the next day I wanted one again, and again Chico lit one for me. This time, though, F. intervened. "Don't smoke," he said in an audible warning from across the lobby. "You're too young." When I hestitated, Chico took the cigarette from my hand and stubbed it out.

Every day after that I cornered someone else in serious pursuit of a cigarette, usually managing a few puffs before F. caught on and made me spit it out. Once he took it out of my mouth himself, looking at me wryly, a cigarette of course between his own lips. He shook his head. "You're too young," he repeated. But by now, I wanted nothing more than a stolen cigarette, smoked brazenly, if possible, in front of F., or, if not, then cadged and smoked on the sly. It began to be a game between us: I would light up whenever I could get one of the older dancers to cooperate with me, and F. would walk over to me, shake his head wearily, and take the cigarette from my mouth.

The contest had been going on for days when our choreography subtly shifted: A slight menace began to color F.'s intervention. Once F. just glared at me without saying anything and angrily pantomimed "Put it out"—I smiled angelically as I relinquished the smoke—and another time he made me raise my foot so he could stub the cigarette out on the sole of my ballet shoe. The game was wordless now: He was beyond telling me that I shouldn't smoke, I was too young, I would ruin my health, I wouldn't be able to breathe, I would hurt my lungs, and so on, all of which washed over me like so much water. Now when I lit up, he simply walked over to me languidly and slapped the cigarette out of my hand, turned his back, and walked away. Someone else—not me, of course, since I wouldn't have deigned—had to retrieve the smoldering cigarette from the floor and extinguish it before the whole ballet studio caught fire. After my cigarette was slapped away, I was more determined than ever.

Mr. Shurbanov tried to broker a truce. He called me over to the piano just before class one day and began to play a few notes of a lovely melody, as if he were doodling on the keyboard. "This music will be for you," he said, intently playing out a tune, "if you give up cigarettes. Please don't smoke," he begged me more fervently, "you're too young, you shouldn't do it, and you're going to make F. very angry. If you stop," he continued, "I promise you I'll compose something beautiful just for you." Mr. Shurbanov's offer took me aback. I was intrigued that he was pleading with me, trying to bribe me, just so that I wouldn't light up. It fascinated me—and also seemed sadly pathetic—that a grown man, an adult, would beg me to give up something for the sake of harmony between myself and my teacher. What was Mr. Shurbanov afraid of? Was he wary of our fireworks? While the lure of music composed for me was enticing, even more so was the idea that there was a vast agon surrounding my attempts to add smoking to my daily routine. Poor, blundering Mr. Shurbanov, trying to be our peacemaker, only raised the stakes.

The next chance I had, I cornered Chico and begged for another cigarette. He turned me down flat. "I don't want to get you into trouble," he said, but what he really meant was that he didn't want to get caught himself in the line of fire. But I pleaded and flirted and cajoled until he acquiesced—on condition that I would meet him surreptitiously in Studio 1, where the younger children practiced and which F. never entered. Chico definitely didn't want to get caught, and since I didn't care much about getting caught but was determined to have my cigarettes, I agreed to Chico's terms. So I sauntered alone into Studio 1 when I thought no one was watching.

The large, rectangular studio had an ell framed by high windows and a window seat; the ell housed the grand piano in back of which Chico and I would be quite securely hidden. Entering the large ballet studio in which I had taken all of my Beginners and Intermediate classes, I realized that it was really quite beautiful, like a stage set of a ballet classroom: the spacious practice space with its parquet floor, wooden barres along three walls, and the immense mirror on the fourth, the ell filled with the grand piano and light streaming in from the high windows. Chico was already there, leaning on the grand piano but still barely visible from the doorway. We parked ourselves on the window seat behind the piano and lit up.

This time Chico was really teaching me; he was serious about my inhaling like an adult, and encouraged me to take long drags on the cigarette. So absorbed were we in our illicit smoke that we hadn't noticed that F. had entered the studio until he was standing practically beside us, next to the grand piano. We jumped to our feet. It was suddenly clear to me that F. must have been tipped off; he couldn't possibly have spotted us, and, anyway, he never, ever, came into this studio. It was also clear to me that our showdown was at hand. I didn't feel guilty or even afraid; I felt exhilarated. F. was smoldering.

He addressed Chico first. "Out," he said, gesturing abruptly toward the door. Chico left, fast. Without saying a word to me, F. held out his hand. I relinquished my cigarette and, with a grimace, he ground it out with his shoe on the parquet floor. Still without saying a word, he motioned to me to turn around so that I was facing the grand piano. He placed both of my hands on the top of the piano, leaned my body against it, and raised his cane.

It seemed to take forever. I could hear the cane traveling toward me, I could feel the air around me displaced by his swing, and I could certainly feel the swift, sharp sting of it. I must have flinched; how could I not? But what I remember is standing there like stone, entirely obedient, even poised, while he struck me three times. What I was aware of most consciously was not the pain and not even the humiliation, but the quality of time, as slow as if we were moving underwater, and the quality of the air, warm and sparkling with dust motes as it spread in waves around me with each arc of the cane. Although I was facing away from F. and couldn't see him, it seemed as if he and I were gracefully synchronized against the backdrop of the grand piano, the man moving slowly and purposefully, the girl posed and still. Not a word was exchanged.

Even now it seems to me a fair bargain: I was forbidden to do something, I insisted on going ahead

almost coolly and without much attempt to camouflage my behavior, and not surprisingly I was caught. I
planned and executed the plot; I was carrying it
through to its natural, inevitable denouement. Daring
begets pain; that was the deal. It was worth it.

There had been a stab of fear for an instant when
Chico left the room. But there was an odd satisfaction,
too, in knowing that what was about to happen with F.
would be private and forbidden, more secret and
taboo than my childish attempts to smoke. Whatever
F. did to me, no one else would ever know: It would
be another bond between us, our secret; we were in
league. I trusted also that retribution would be quick,
inevitable, and elegant, as indeed it was.

Nevertheless there were limits. F. seemed to be
waiting for me to cry out, but that far I wouldn't go: I
would take it, whatever he meted out, and agree
within myself that such a punishment was fair and
just, but I would not ask for it, and I certainly would
not directly acknowledge his power with a plea to stop
or a cry of pain. If he was brutally deliberate in station-
ing me as if I were at the barre in order to take better
aim, I would be poised and elegant in return, not giving in to alarm or distress for an instant, even though
each stroke took my breath away. The reciprocity was
perfect.

When he finished, I turned around to look at F.,
catching my breath. Courteous as always, he gave me a

little ironic bow as if to say, *Thank you*. I just looked at him, feeling nothing, not even relief that the drama was over. For a few moments my body had been his; it had been bruised and owned by someone else. Now it was mine again, and I almost didn't know what to do with it, except to stare at him and feel wrenched back into the present, the studio, the classroom, with Chico lurking about somewhere, guiltily imagining what was happening to me.

F. took a step backward, creating a narrow aisle between himself and the piano; he motioned gracefully to me to leave, to precede him out of the room, as courteously as if he were holding open a door.

But what happened next was inexplicable to me, unheard of. As I passed in front of him, walking out of the studio with my best and totally ingrained ballet posture, F. hit me one more time with such ferocity that the blow swung me around. I whirled around to face him. *That* was not part of the bargain, not part of the deal, not part of the reciprocity of elegance and pain we had so perfectly enacted. It was entirely unfair, uncalled for, and very, very painful. I was so amazed and hurt I couldn't speak. For the first time in all of our encounters, I had to choke back tears. Rather than cry in front of him, I fled to the dressing room without looking back.

That last stroke shattered our agreement, the secret understanding we had forged between us. The violence was clearly superfluous, excessive, a sign that some mania for punishment had taken over F., unbalancing his usual methodic calculation of the ratio of pain to pleasure. Certainly the superfluous violence broke through my confidence, my sense that I could steer F. toward me and away from me, at my own pleasure. Even now I can remember the feeling of dissolving, of the treacherous loss of my willpower, the loss of my resolve to keep still, poised, even dignified in the face of F.'s retaliation. When I fled the room I wasn't afraid. I didn't look back to see if F. was still angry or if he was surprised at my running off, nor did I for a second expect him to pursue me, either to hit me again or to apologize. But I was stunned. Had I been a real person, I might have said to myself, *He shouldn't have done that.* But I was a dancer so I said nothing, even to myself; I instead retreated as quickly as I could into a vague, numb world in which sensation—feeling—does not exist.

For some time afterward I avoided F. as much as I could, even though I was still in class with him every day. But I didn't look at him, didn't try to catch his eye, didn't try to coax or tease out attention from him; I just went about my ballet exercises as if by remote control. I felt whitened, blanked out, as if someone had passed an eraser over me and had left a flat, chalky space where my body used to be. F., too, was just a thin, faceless shadow, a gray streak moving soundlessly around the studio.

Little by little, when nothing further happened and daily class began to feel like business as usual, I realized with surprise that F. was avoiding me as much as I was trying to obliterate him. He didn't want to look me in the eye either or come too close. We had each—at least for a while—reined in our impetuousness, that craving for connection that had led me to taunt him with my cigarettes and that had led him to track me down and overstep the boundaries we had tacitly agreed on. We became quiescent; a torpor fell between us. For awhile I could be just another dancer, almost anonymous, placidly standing in line with all the other girls at the barre.

I didn't lose my desire for cigarettes, although I no longer had the impulse to smoke brazenly in front of F. Instead for years afterward, whenever I lit a cigarette and placed it in my mouth, I felt the lure of the forbidden, the thrill of taunting authority, the peculiar sensation of knowing that I might be cornered and punished. The anger at how unjust it was. Even now, my body hasn't forgotten: Just thinking about smoking makes me involuntarily shiver.

When we finally returned to "full company" rehearsals, something magical had happened: Somehow we had taken these random pieces of choreography and made them into a full ballet, a nineteenth-century classic, an

enchanting and lighthearted love story. Our Swanhilda, a small blond dancer named Gioconda, was
adorable and had perfect comic timing; her "friends"
danced all around her, and we corps de ballet girls were
transformed from naive students into happy, high-
spirited villagers who just felt like tossing off a mazurka
or a czardas with energetic abandon. I couldn't wait to
get into my costume and onstage.

I loved the costume—the colorful skirt that swirled
around my knees as I turned, the white peasant
blouse, and laced-up black bodice. Best of all were the
chunky-heeled shoes for the jumps, slides, and heel
clicks of character dancing. Wearing flowers in our
hair and with everything about us jolly and gay, we
were merrily robust peasants, not wraiths or swans or
sylphs or even little ballet girls. All of us villagers
shared a large communal dressing room underneath
the stage, where we put on our makeup and did our
hair. We camped out there until just before curtain,
when it was time to troop into the wardrobe room,
where the costume ladies would fit us into our peasant
dresses. Each dress had a name tag on it; one of the
wardrobe women would find it in the row of similar
dresses, lift it off its hanger and slip it over the
dancer's head, quickly hooking it up in the back. Just
as we peasants were leaving for the wardrobe room,
Sonya dropped in and clapped her hands for our
attention.

"Girls," she announced, "remember to be absolutely silent on your way to wardrobe and everywhere backstage. *No talking,* repeat, *no talking* backstage. Mazurka girls, someone will come for you. I'll meet you backstage and get you lined up in the wings. When the mazurka is over, go directly back down to your dressing room and stay there. Third-act czardas girls will get a call. Remember, *no talking*."

No talking was fine with me. Even though initially we had all been full of high spirits and chatter as we arrived at the theater, as it got closer to curtain time we had all fallen silent. Silent with stage fright, that dizzying feeling of terror, nausea in the pit of the stomach, and intense total concentration on the small task at hand, whether it is pulling on your tights, checking your shoes, or applying makeup. Number two greasepaint, flesh tone, squeezed out of a tube. Rouge. Eyeliner and thick, false eyelashes glued to the lids. A small dab of white at the inner and outer corners of the eyes to make them sparkle in the bright stage lights. But utter silence, concentration, terror.

On the other hand, I didn't want to perform my mazurka and exit the stage only to return to a cavernous dressing room as if I were under the eyes of a strict governess; I wanted to watch from the wings as the whole ballet unfolded. I even wanted to watch Tina dance her role as Swanhilda's friend, so no matter what Sonya had said, I was filled with chagrin and disappointment to find that I would be spending the entire performance in my dressing room, except for my few moments onstage. I was too inexperienced to realize that Sonya was demanding of us standard stage etiquette: The wings are not social clubs for unoccupied dancers watching their friends. Backstage, as I only fully realized much later, is a city, a world unto itself, more populous and sometimes with even better choreography for its crowds than the intricate dancing out front seen by the audience. Everything backstage must run according to strict plan, under the aegis of the stage manager whose word is law: No one stands around who isn't needed, and traffic flows in patterns as carefully determined as on the grid of any city. Dancers scheduled to appear in that night's performance appear backstage only a few moments before the opening notes of the music that heralds their entrance; otherwise they wait, warming up and jittery with nerves, until the bell in their dressing room calls them to the wings. If they are not scheduled to dance until late in the evening, they might not even arrive at the theater until the curtain rises and the first ballet is under way.

With my costume finally hooked securely, my character shoes making rhythmic clicking noises on the floor, I lined up backstage with the other villagers. Under Sonya's directions we waited silently, in terror, for our entry. Then as if from nowhere we heard the jolting first notes of our music and flew onstage. Suddenly I was breathless, as if I had been shot out of a cannon, but there I was, onstage and performing, whirling around and stamping my heels with the other peasants. The heat was overwhelming, the lights were blinding—and the noise! Who would have thought that a stage would be such a cacophonous space? But torrents of sound swelled from all directions, from the orchestra, from our shoes and the men's boots, even from the swish of our skirts as they swirled around.

And then, just as abruptly, it was all over. There was a surge of applause from the audience as we rushed off, and all of a sudden there I was panting in the wings, my mouth dry and sweat pouring off me. But *Coppelia* of course was continuing, and I instantly knew that this was what I had come for—to stand still and watch, revel in the rest of the performance, the friends, the pantomime, Swanhilda's variation, Franz falling in love with the doll Coppelia, mistaking her for a real maiden. I pressed myself into the edge of the wings, stagestruck with fascination.

In a moment Sonya was beside me, waving at me to get moving downstairs to the dressing room as I had been told. I ignored her. The last thing I wanted to do was to leave the performance. "To your dressing room," she whispered urgently. I shook my head, mesmerized by the dancing, the dancers usually so grimy and fatigued from endless rehearsals now luminous with costumes, makeup, new satin pointe shoes, glistening with sweat under the hot lights and dancing ferociously.

"Downstairs!" Sonya commanded, slightly raising her voice and motioning with her arms as if she were a broom sweeping me along in front of her. Again I shook my head, eyes glued to the stage.

Then Sonya stood directly in front of me, blocking my view. *"To your dressing room—"* she urged, loud enough to be heard over Delibes's score. "I told you. *Move!"*

But I barely saw her: I practically erased her from my vision. All I could see was the lovely dancing; all I could hear was the orchestra, its lyrical strings and piccolos as Swanhilda and her friends planned to invade the toyshop of old Dr. Coppelius. Every moment, every step of the ballet I had learned; I could have walked out onto the stage and performed anyone's role, from Swanhilda's to each of the mechanical dolls, to old, gnarled Dr. Coppelius himself, shielding Coppelia, his own precious mechanical doll, from wayward lovers like the oafish Franz. What did it matter if I was boy or girl, doll or dancer, as long as I was onstage, dancing my heart out? And if I couldn't do that, I'd stay in the wings watching hungrily, devouring the ballet. What difference could one person make? I was small, practically invisible.

"Shhhhhh," I whispered uneasily to Sonya, my finger over my mouth. Hadn't we been told not to talk in the wings? I myself was utterly quiet, trying to look straight through Sonya as if she were transparent. Sonya moved in closer to me, but I wouldn't budge. If I had really looked at her, noticed her, taken my eyes from the stage for one second to pay any attention at all, I would have seen that Sonya was glowering with rage, but I had waited for so long for these moments of utterly joyous performance, with music—real music!—booming from the orchestra pit and the heady sensation of an audience as if it were some immense animal out there in the darkness, clapping and breathing in unison, and the dancers swirling and glistening in the heat, that Sonya was just an irritation, like a flea or mosquito. Almost absentmindedly, I was trying to swat her away.

It unnerves me to admit this even now, but Sonya struck me as powerless; she made no difference to me. I was smaller than Sonya, true, and much, much younger—only fourteen—but where Sonya was concerned I must have felt myself omnipotent. That's the only way I can explain to myself what happened next— that compared to Sonya, I felt myself charmed and powerful. All those instances of taking food practically from her mouth! Of listening to F.'s wry complaints about wives, of observing his disdain and disregard for his third one. I must have thought that no matter what I did, I would be protected by F. who was my beacon and lodestar. Who preferred me above all others. Who certainly preferred me to his chunky wife.

"Get out of my way!" I suddenly find myself ordering Sonya, shocking myself with a voice that is no longer a backstage whisper but loud and compelling enough to be heard onstage, in the audience, probably even out in the streets. *"You're blocking my view."*

Sonya reared back as if I had struck her, hesitated a second, and then with a fleeting grimace of surprise she quickly disappeared.

The corps de ballet dressing room, when I returned to it after the curtain finally fell, was almost empty. Makeup and bathrobes were strewn everywhere, but all the costumes had been returned to the wardrobe room and the one or two villagers still dallying over getting into their street clothes were packing up their dance cases ready to leave the theater. As quickly as I could, I stepped out of my costume, hung it on its hanger for the wardrobe mistress to collect, and rubbed the heavy makeup from my face with cold cream. The soloists were chatting in their own dressing room next door as I left, but the stage was dark and lights were off in the maze of unused hallways beneath the stage. Sonya was nowhere to be seen, and F., who had been tensely jubilant backstage during curtain calls, had disappeared as well. I had the vague sense that something was amiss but I couldn't quite figure out what it was.

The next night we repeated *Coppelia* and the third night after that as well. Each night after my own quick dancing with the corps de ballet I hid myself in the wings to watch the rest of the performance. As the dancers hurled themselves offstage whizzing by me in the air or landing practically right on top of me, I flattened myself farther into the wing to avoid getting trampled, but as long as I caused no accidents no one paid any attention to me or even seemed to notice that I was there. No one any longer blocked my view; for the rest of the performances I had the wing all to myself. Sonya when she passed alongside me ignored me as if I were air.

I've won, I told myself. *I've been able to drink in the whole ballet, to see every step and nuance.* F. would be on my side, I was sure, even against Sonya. Hadn't he been outraged when I had failed at understudying? I kept reminding myself that I was a younger, more promising, and probably even better dancer than Sonya, that I had my future before me and was not going to settle for being a teacher of Intermediate Class, that I brought F. more pleasure than she could. . . . Didn't he always feed me at her expense, lavish attention on me, and burn with irritation at Sonya when she intruded?

And yet at each performance I felt just the slightest bit more uneasy, although I would not for anything have given up my spot in the wings. As far as I was concerned, that little square foot of stage where I stood each night had my name engraved on it.

"Martine!" I called out gaily, dashing into the dressing room at the ballet school a little late for our first class after *Coppelia*. "Did you see the reviews?"

Martine shook her head. "Mmmm," she mumbled. "Got to go." Slinging her dance case over one shoulder and grabbing her towel and pointe shoes, Martine headed for the hallway. *Rush!* I ordered myself, peeling off my street clothes and jerking on my tights and leotard as fast as possible. I, too, hoisted my dance case over a shoulder, tightening the hairpins around my bun as I headed quickly into the studio.

Taking my usual place at the barre next to Martine, I began to stretch, whispering to Martine at the same time. Wasn't that photo of Swanhilda and Franz in the betrothal scene just hilarious? He looked so idiotically lovestruck . . . but her arabesque was good, didn't she think? Martine gave me a funny look. Then, turning her back to me, she slid down to the floor in a wide split. Just at that moment, F. entered and rapped on the floor with his cane to begin the class.

I stayed after class for awhile to work on my pirouettes; as usual, they hadn't been steady enough, although F. hadn't noticed. He had concentrated that day on Martine, who was in a visibly cheerful mood as

F. acerbically teased and bullied her into dancing even better than usual. She was never limber enough, she thought, and sometimes shoved her body into painful contortions in the attempt to make herself more elastic, but today she was particularly pliant and light, as if some of the performing spirit from *Coppelia* had stayed with her. She wore makeup, too—the lipstick and eyeliner highlighting her dark, slanted eyes and wide mouth—and no one threw *her* out of class. Martine looks *professional*, I suddenly realized, with a stab of jealousy.

The next day before class a knot of girls glanced at me strangely when I entered the dressing room to change, huddling together and whispering to each other. Martine, too, was remote, almost unfriendly, and had left her usual place at the barre next to me for another spot on the opposite side of the room. When I guardedly whispered to her during class to ask what was wrong, she acted as if she didn't hear me and turned away.

Again F. directed his attention to Martine and the other girls, as if he hadn't noticed how I was dancing. It crossed my mind that he might be ignoring me, just as the girls seemed deliberately to be paying no attention me, but I blotted out that suspicion as impossible. Hadn't he always watched me like a hawk, corrected everything, never let the least misstep or sloppiness on my part go undetected?

I decided to test F.'s attention. Willfully I made some small error. No reaction. Minutes later I deliberately flubbed something else, substituting altogether different steps in a dance combination as if I had forgotten the choreography and were forced to improvise. Again no reaction from F., nothing. Was I formless? Invisible? Was there a tent of darkness around me that erased my presence?

After class no one spoke to me. The girls in the dressing room busied themselves with their hair or their shoes whenever I started a conversation, and Martine insulated herself from me in their midst. Suddenly it dawned on me: No one had willingly said a word to me in two days. They all seemed to have made a pact to ignore me, to pretend that I didn't exist.

I decided that I would pretend that all was normal; I would go on as if I hadn't noticed a thing about my friends' strange behavior and, in any case, couldn't have cared less. But suddenly Martine came toward me, for the first time in two days of her own volition. "I have to talk to you," she whispered, her finger over her mouth warning me to be quiet. "But we can't do it here."

"Where?" I mouthed.

Five minutes later we meet in the girls' bathroom, where, huddled in a stall so that we are hidden from view, Martine quickly informs me that F. has called all the girls together and given them an order: Everyone is forbidden to talk to me. "Not a word," he said.

"He told you that?" I ask, thunderstruck. "Why?"

Martine shrugs; she doesn't know. F. hadn't explained; he had only said, mysteriously, "She's not a good girl, she's bad," and that was it. Martine imitates him shaking his head mournfully. "She's bad." Martine would be in trouble if anyone caught her talking to me, so she'd better go. And with that she guiltily lets herself out of the bathroom, looking around to make sure that no one has seen her. "Look right, look left—maybe F. is around, yes?"

Martine didn't understand the edict, but I did. Suddenly everyone's turning away from me made perfect sense: ". . . not a good girl," F. had said. "Don't talk to her." It was my punishment for disobeying Sonya, for refusing to leave the wings like the good corps de ballet girl I was supposed to be.

Punishment by silence. Day after day the silence continued.

For me the whole world has been stilled.

Days follow in a slow blur of silence, as if we are all moving underwater, dancing through our classes and gesturing to each other with slow heavy ripples of arms and legs undulating in the viscous water. I vaguely sense bubbles in the water surrounding me when the girls speak to one another, waves breaking gently around me as they move and gesture, but no one speaks to me; my world is viscous, greenish, full of shadows, and totally silent. When I dance I can barely hear the piano music; somewhere in the room Mr. Shurbanov pounds his keys as always, but the sounds are only echoes and vibrations coming at me as if from very far away, through layers and layers of waves. Even F. himself cannot see me, immersed as I am in the waters of silence. Whatever I do makes no difference: I can dance what the other girls are dancing or make up chains of steps entirely on my own, dance brilliantly or hideously; it does not matter. No one pays the slightest attention to me. I am invisible even to F.

But I persist. I change from my street clothes to my practice clothes and from my practice clothes to my street clothes in my silent cell in the dressing room, go to the barre with everyone else, try to pay attention in class to F.'s choreography and corrections as if they might be meant for me, even though they clearly are not and I have been erased from everyone's vision. I try to be nonchalant, but in my few moments of lucidity I am stunned by my own fear and, even, by my own anger: *Quarantine,* I say to myself. *Ostracism. Excommunication.* I have heard about these kinds of punishments before, in military schools and in monasteries. *What is this, boot camp?* I say bitterly to myself. *Am I a marine? Am I a novice in a medieval convent whose identity needs be stripped away to bring her closer to*

God? After a while I devise a sullen litany for myself. *I am being ostracized,* I think over and over. *I am being ostracized. I am in exile.*

The silent treatment is meant to break me, I realize, and it works. Sometimes I think, *Eventually this will be over. He will call me into his office and wreck some havoc upon me, inflict pain, damage me. Good, let him.* And then I think, *This will go on forever. F. will never notice me again.* A moment later, the opposite thought: *This can't go on.* I don't think these thoughts serially, but rather simultaneously, as if one thought were layered on the other, one thought on its contradictory thought, in layer upon layer of confusion and contradiction and all stifling me at once. Just as torture and self-mutilation once worked, were efficacious in making me a dancer, silence is taking it all away from me, gradually stripping me from myself until there is nothing left.

Quite soon, within days or maybe only hours or minutes, I am invisible not only to F. and everyone else around me but invisible as well to myself. I can look at my right arm moving through *port de bras* and not even see it. When I look in the mirror there is nothing there, no one staring back at me with her head tilted Kirov-style and her legs scissoring beautifully through the air.

There can be no dancer without a body, no dance when all the chords and trills and hums of vitality are muted, extinguished, silenced. Disembodied, I no longer exist.

While I am dressing after class as quickly as possible inside my cave of silence, standing far apart from the other girls who haven't chanced a word to me in days, I hear a voice that sounds vaguely familiar. Because I have not risked a conversation either, I don't answer; I have lost the ability to speak. Nor can I see who is speaking to me, as if the silence surrounding me for days has not only numbed but blinded me. But I listen, faintly awestruck at the sound of a human voice actually piercing my quarantine and making its strange melodic way into my consciousness. It's my name. Someone is actually calling me. It takes me a moment or two longer to realize that the voice is Astrid's: She has a message—again, a familiar one. F. wants to see me. Right away, now. In his secret room.

I don't hesitate. I have been waiting for this moment. I knew it would happen, that F. would finally call me, summon me, let me know what fate, what final retribution, he has decided for me. I start up the staircase and down the long hall toward his secret room, knowing that what will happen to me on the other side of his door is anyone's guess, that I will open that door and step into a yawning pit of flames and fury, that I will be charred beyond recognition simply by a glance, an ironic comment, a swift slash of his leather cane against my body.

I am hoping for no less. He can lash me to shreds: I deserve it. "She is bad," he has told everyone, and only I know how right he is, how little I cared for the consequences of my disobedience, how much I enjoyed pitting myself against his wife and telling her off. "You're blocking my view," I had said gleefully, and now I saw how true that was: She had been blocking my view, had stood in my way, had underestimated my ambition, my desire. She had been blocking my view for years. And I had dispatched her, had blown her into smithereens, crazily confident that F. would be on my side. I had thought, deep down, that he would choose me.

But the silence has taught me differently. He won't choose me at all, I have lost, and I don't know what will happen. Whatever happens will be terrible, but I don't know what it will be. An inchoate desire for immolation is careening around in my head—I want it, I can't bear it!—and I am suddenly filled with nausea and begin to black out. I double over, jack-knifed at the waist. The vertigo passes, and I go into his room quickly, without hesitation. Without even knocking. To get it over with.

Surprisingly, F. is seated formally at his desk. The desk, even though it has been in his secret room all along, I have never before thought of as simply what it is: a desk. F. and I have always used it for something else—a table for our cheese and vodka, a platform for me to sit on, feet up and my arms hugging my knees while we talk. If I mocked him, he would swivel me around by the shoulders until I was pressed against it and would, almost teasingly, flick me with his cane. But now he just motions to me to come stand beside the desk, and then he stares straight ahead. Not at me.

He looks miserable.

"You are expelled," he says finally, still staring into space and speaking so quietly I have to strain to hear him. "For disobeying orders. And you were rude to my wife." He sounds ceremoniously formal, as if he is a general talking to an orderly. Where had he learned this strange language, this stilted multisyllabic English that is not ballet talk, not Russian curses, not the whistling I am used to from this man? How could he sit so quietly when he should be roaming the room, preparing my tumbler of ginger ale, raising his glass to me in an affectionate toast?

As if in a military tribunal, I stand rigidly beside the desk while F., not looking at me, pronounces my sentence. When he finishes he glances at me sadly and nods. "You can go," he adds when I don't move.

I can go. I don't argue; I haven't said a word the entire time.

During this encounter F. has looked at me only once, telling me at the end of his speech that I can leave, although I have not for a second taken my eyes from him. Watching him stare unhappily out into space while he pronounces my expulsion, I wish that he would look at me. Really look at me. And then come at me, threaten me. Stand up, press me against the desk, raise his cane and hit with me it, as much as he wishes, again and again. The pain, the sting of it, mean nothing to me. After a week of silence, I need some contact with him, some biting dramatic moment of pain and surrender. Not only mine but his. Not this emptiness, this melancholy formality and silence. It is the emptiness more than anything that tells me that my time is up.

But although I have never, ever admitted it to myself before this moment, secretly I agree with him.

He's right, I can go, I think, facing F. in complete silence. *If I don't get out now, I never will.* It's not that I have had enough of F., that I am "over" him: I will never get over him, never. I know, even though I have danced for a week under an avalanche of utter silence, that I can never get enough of his strange, damaged, ironic yearning over me, the caresses of his hands or the flicks of his cane, his vodka raised in a toast, the hidden suffocating gorgeousness of his secret room that only I visit.

But the danger is—and suddenly I see it so clearly—that I am on the brink of not only becoming a dancer, but becoming a dancer whose life is devoted to F., whose every aspect of being is entirely in his hands.

I know those hands: They have given me everything I have, great and wonderful gifts. He has thrown me into the air, spun me around, molded my body, made my arabesque into arrows shooting up into the heavens. My leg is straight in *battement tendu*, I can spin like a top in *chainé* turns even when my hands aren't bloodied. I can work with a man, a partner, breathe when he does, count when he does, get myself up into the air and back down again. I can dance the pas de deux from *Les Sylphides* with anyone. Even more, F. has bequeathed me his volatile, lyrical ballet style, his Russian "line" as well as his Russian soul and madness; his melodies are whistling in my head. I share his belief that the way to conquer space is to hurl yourself through it.

And yet if I stay with F., if I don't get out while I can, I might well become another Astrid, hanging onto F.'s gestures, an adoring acolyte forever. Or another Sonya, bitterly kneading my calves after a long day doing *changements* with little girls, eating chocolates for solace. No matter how much he is adored, a ballet master requires a ballet slave.

I want what I have always wanted: to dance, to *become* a dancer, and the best one I could possibly be, at any cost, at whatever price that ambition exacted. To learn new ballets, to feel the chords and rhythms of music coursing through my sinews, to gulp huge drafts of air into my lungs when I performed some feat I had once thought impossible, to have a body perfectly trained as a melodious instrument for a great classical tradition.

He is right, I should be expelled. I deserve it. Not so much for disobeying Sonya—who cares about Sonya!—but for secretly agreeing with him that I should go. For still wanting more than anything to be a dancer, even if that means parting from F. forever.

Once—so long ago, it seems now—he had said to me, "Your parents or me. You have to choose." F.'s edict, given centuries ago when I was twelve, pronounced as if eons back in my far-off childhood, careens through my memory. Always his words had haunted me. I had chosen him instantaneously, without hesitation, and had cast aside everyone else whom I loved to cleave to F. and make of him a universe— my family, my teacher, my lover, my friend, my whole world. Now, standing in disgrace at F.'s desk in his secret room, I saw that F. was forcing me once again to make a choice.

This time I choose to give him up. *If I stay here I'll die,* I think. *Now is the moment, right now—I can go.*

Without saying a word, without even a gesture that I have heard him, I turn around, let myself out of the room, and close the door behind me.

When I leave his secret room, I know that it is the final moment for me there, that no matter what happens to me in the future, I will never again be alone with F., the door closed behind us, in his room where anything can happen. Where we dance our gavotte of power and submission, where I can get him to regard me ironically and raise his cane against me to keep me at bay, as if otherwise I might leap at him. It is the right time to go.

So I left him. But not with any anticipation of a wonderful future, not with any sense of release.

I left his office, went back downstairs to the girls' dressing room and curled up on a bench in a far corner of the room, as if I were a sick animal left alone to die. All that bravado flashing through my head in the moment F. expelled me, all that certainty about being able to leave F., give him up for good—what was I thinking? Not to see F. every day, not to wait at the barre for him to enter the studio whistling, debonair, his bow tie slightly askew? Not to feel that thrill of trepidation, of surrender to anything asked of me in his secret room? I felt bludgeoned, stunned: I really had been expelled, no matter whether it was the right time to go or not. No matter that I deserved it, no matter that indeed I had earned the right to leave, to move on—that if I hadn't been expelled, I would have had to part from F. anyway, of my own volition, for my own good. No matter that I would never apologize to Sonya, never make peace with F., never ask him to take me back or try to win him over again, and that I would now choose to give up the very man to whom I had devoted every atom of my being.

I sat numbed and motionless for a long time. Finally I roused myself, packed up my dance case with my practice clothes, ballet shoes, towel, took a last look around the dressing room, went upstairs, walked past F.'s office, which was silent. The studios were silent; the building seemed to be empty. I saw no one, so without fanfare I left. I would never see this studio again.

Twelve, thirteen, fourteen. By the time I was fourteen it was all over. One life.

What happened, really?

A man chose me, singled me out, called me to come to him. He trained me and taught me everything I wanted to know. He touched me; he adjusted my wrist, my arm, the tilt of my head, so that I became beautiful, so that I saw how beautiful a dancer could be, a woman could be in her body. He fed me chocolates and ginger ale; he lifted me into the air. I performed for him exuberantly but also with fear, as he wished. He knew he could do anything to me. He knew I would do anything for him. When he was angry, he cursed me in Russian, and even his insults I desired. He let other men touch me, but only when he

Solo

watched. When we were alone, he hit me. I became
his, forsaking all others.

What happened, really?

A man chose me from among several others,
because I was more dedicated, more talented, more
hardworking. Maybe he chose me only because he
knew I wanted him to. In the age-old tradition of classical ballet, especially as practiced in czarist Russia and
well into the twentieth century, he allowed me to
apprentice myself to him, to study in his class every
day. He taught me ballet technique, both fundamen-
tals and the more indefinable elements of style. From
him, I learned the choreography of some of the great
ballets: *Les Sylphides*, *Sleeping Beauty*, *Coppelia*. He was
strict and demanding, although no more so than other
renowned ballet teachers; he was also cynical and
remote. He often humiliated me; he seemed to enjoy
it. In the end he expelled me from his school. Perhaps
he let me go because I was less promising and less talented than he had thought, or because I interposed
myself between him and his wife. Perhaps I had
become a "heavy ballerina," someone a man had to lug
around the stage. Perhaps he just got bored with me.
In ballet, there is always another girl—young, thin,
promising, malleable, driven—waiting in the wings,
waiting to be chosen. A younger girl, willing to do
anything.

What happened, really?

For three years in my early teens, I studied ballet
with F., a renowned and demanding teacher who mesmerized me. When I had learned everything I could
from him, we parted abruptly, on bad terms. I went on
to other teachers, joined a ballet company, and encountered F. only once more before he died. I *think* he
remembered me, but possibly he did not.

All three of these versions are true. But it is the
third, of course, that makes the most sense to me now,
the most realistic, pared-down version, shorn of mys-
tery, metaphor, romance. The story that tells me I was
never to F. what I had thought I was, the girl he would
make a star. This is the version that allows me to ease
into normalcy, into real life.

It is years later. I am going about my normal, everyday,
ordinary life, trying to be like everyone else, erasing as
much as possible everything about my dancer's life
that doesn't fit tongue and groove into explainable
reality. Somehow (I am not sure how or when), along
a trajectory of ordinary life, I have become a real person. Not a dancer any longer. "Give it up cold turkey,"
dancers say. I follow their wisdom: There is not a *plié*
in my life or I would be lost for good.

I allow, I *urge* the sinews and humming molecules
of my body to "forget" the ballet world as much as
possible: My now unremarkable body goes on its

everyday path as a nondancer, a former dancer. I have lost touch with Martine as if she never existed, and Astrid, if I think about her at all, must still be at F.'s ballet school teaching Beginners Class, arranging her hair in the big mirror of her dressing room, chatting warily with Sonya, fetching a pack of cigarettes for Mr. Shurbanov, unless he, too, is dead. The ballerina charm Astrid clasped around my neck—the tiny ballerina pivoting on one sharp toe in arabesque—has somehow disappeared into thin air; I cannot even remember taking it off.

I have even thrown away my first pair of blood-stained pointe shoes that I had been keeping in the bottom of my closet as a memento. When I came across them one day, I couldn't believe I had treasured them for so long as if they were relics. They had hardened over the years but were still pliable, still softly fragrant with sweat and resin, but there seemed to be no reason any longer to hold on to them, so I tucked them into the day's garbage as if I were hiding forbidden treasure. Afterward I was half sorry and wished I had at least swaddled them in tissue paper to toss them out.

But in the most private depths of memory I continue to harbor F., savoring and tormenting myself with images of the relationship long after it in fact has ended. He exists for me indelibly—in chains of unforgotten events that I can recall the way I remember choreography: A note of music heard or a ballet step casually marked brings back the entire sequence, etched in the innermost fibers of my dancer's body.

Sometime in my late twenties, I saw F. for the last time. Even though I had not been in a ballet studio or on stage for a few years, I decided to go to a ballet performance to see if I could allow myself that small dram of pleasure without again surrendering myself to addiction. To see if I could, with ease, be a spectator rather than the girl in the corps de ballet of *Les Sylphides* or *Swan Lake*, shoving her pointe shoes into the resin box a second before the bars of her music; whirling or leaping offstage into the wings, her mouth dry and her chest heaving, taking company curtain calls and then leaving the theater at midnight, exhausted and exhilarated, for dinner.

Instead I ran into F. He was with a small group of men and women, none of whom I had ever seen before, all of them seemingly former dancers, ancient, aged, over-the-hill dancers, talking quietly and companionably. I hesitated for a moment and then approached him.

F. glanced up, greeted me by name, and drew me into his circle, but he was neither effusive nor particularly welcoming, nor was he, as I might have expected had I thought about it, the slightest bit angry or sardonic. We chatted politely about what I was doing, but whatever we said was compelling to neither of us.

Courtly as ever, he offered me a cigarette. When I accepted, he got out the silver cigarette lighter I knew so well from years of watching him smoke, of scrutinizing his every gesture and responding to it. With utmost politeness but complete indifference, he leaned toward me and lit my cigarette. I remembered that years earlier he had forbidden me to smoke—and that when he had caught me with a cigarette, flagrantly defiant, he had beaten me methodically and with unusual brutality. And now he was offering me another one, casually, one adult to another. It was the saddest thing in the world, that cigarette. It meant I was no longer a dancer, a child star, in danger, his beloved: I had moved away.

Coda

$\mathcal{H}$ow could I have left F., whom I adored beyond belief? How could I have just walked out, down the concrete steps of the ballet school and out onto the sidewalk, how could I have boarded my usual bus home for the last time and paid my ordinary fare, my ballet case slung over one shoulder as it always was, with not one look back at the man left behind in our secret room at the studio? I didn't look back, not for one second, not ever.

But I couldn't stop myself from thinking about him. What was F. doing, what was he thinking, as I left? Did he just sit still at his desk, listening for my footsteps as I walked away from him down the hall, out of the building forever? Was he sorry, did he suddenly shake his head in disbelief at what he had done, at how quickly he had thrown me out, at letting me go so easily? Was he dismayed that I hadn't argued with him, hadn't pleaded with him to be allowed to remain on whatever terms he decreed, that I hadn't begged to stay on? Shouldn't I have said, as dancers always do, *Sorry. Sorry, my fault*?

It never occurred to me to apologize. Instead, what I really wanted to say was, *Thank you. Thank you for letting me go.*

The beginning of love, its genesis, is clear—often strikingly clear—but the way love ends is mysterious, unfathomable.

I can't tell, even now, if I left F. or if he left me. Perhaps that's the way of all love stories: They just end, with no one truly comprehending his or her role in the inevitability of parting. You leave someone forever or someone leaves you, and you have only the faintest idea of why or how it happened. All you really know is that the love is over.

After F. expelled me, I went home. A strange idea. For such a long time—decades, it seemed—I hadn't been home without the knowledge that in a few hours I would turn around and return to ballet school. Return to F. This time it was really *home*: where I lived, where my family occupied the rooms, the place I could return to as a sanctuary even though in every way I felt homeless, even abandoned. I went into my bedroom, closed the door, lay down on my bed and tried to cry. I wanted to burst into tears at my loss, I wanted to exhaust myself with torrents of tears, but the truth is that I could not cry at all.

Instead I was steely, cold. I had to make plans, move on, find another way to keep dancing, find myself another ballet home, another place to take class, another teacher, a new ballet company. An hour later I was on the phone with the secretary of a ballet company—a fledgling company I had heard of from the older girls in *Coppelia* but had not yet seen. I scheduled an audition for myself the following day.

Introducing myself to the director of this new ballet company for a quick, private class, I did a few warm-up exercises at the barre, a few pirouettes and *chainé* turns, an adagio in the center. I think I must have seemed feverish, desperate. But I was taken in. By the following weekend I was rehearsing the *pas de quatre*, the dance of the cygnets, from *Swan Lake*, and by the weekend after that I had been cast in two more ballets in the corps de ballet.

But I knew almost immediately that my life in this new ballet company, no matter how rewarding it would be to practice and perform, would be on a diminished plane: There was no F. He was gone from my world, he had erased himself from it, and there could be no replacement. I would have no more of his toxic, exhilarating daily presence, no more private (or public) beatings, no more hours spent lounging in his secret room, drinking ginger ale and listening to stories of great dancers he had taught, no more uneasy viewings of the snapshot F. liked to force me to look at, of how he could control a ballerina with one hand.

I didn't miss F. in the ordinary sense in which one longs for and thinks about a person lost. What I felt at first was gradual relief, as if for the first time in years I could breathe openly and easily. In the new ballet company, no one was watching me with any but the most ordinary interest; no one was calculating, assessing, judging, calibrating my ratio of fear to bravado. No one cared whether or not I was a "great dancer." Clearly I wasn't one. Another girl was the star, the teacher's pet, the beloved. Instead I just took my two classes a day and danced in the corps de ballet, along with everyone else.

Martine joined me, finally, months later. I never found out how—or why—she left F., but one day there she was, at the barre in the midst of all of my new friends and then in the new ballet company. But something had blunted our friendship; I never quite knew what it was. Perhaps with Martine I was still under an edict of silence, a ban. Perhaps Martine remembered F.'s words—"she's bad"—and still didn't dare to talk to me.

But sometimes we exchanged a complicit look, a glance of comprehension, some wordless gesture that we both could recognize: *This isn't the same,* we signaled to each other. *We're doing the steps, but this isn't really dancing. Not like it was with F.* We both knew what it was like to dance our hearts out, dance to exhaustion, dance to express an idea, a feeling, a longing, or a promise. *I love you with all my heart—Do you see?—I am making a vow to you, an eternal vow. Now let's dance together; take my hand. Yes, we will dance until we die.*

I never talked with Martine about the secret room, never mentioned F.'s name. Even though the memories of that room gave me intense private pleasure, I knew that if I told anyone—even someone as sympathetic and knowledgeable about F. as Martine—I would be faced with uneasy questions that for years I could not have begun to answer. Why *did* a grown man repeatedly take a thirteen-year-old girl into a back room, for example? Another one: Why did this man lie down and methodically whip himself with his cane when what he so clearly wanted was a confrontation with me? When I would have acquiesced in anything he wished? Once I learned—years later in the motel room with the man I was in love with—the startling answers to my questions, my ostracism ended, the ban of silence lifted. Then I could have talked to Martine. Because I knew, for the first time, the real nature of my connection to F. Martine would have understood immediately, as would any other dancer, that ballet breeds its own love stories: love stories that are not found openly in the real world.

Perhaps because I didn't tell these stories about F. for such a long time, I sometimes can recall nothing, as if long ago the synapses of memory had permanently snapped. More often I remember an event, a scene, a mood, with more clarity than I feel I can bear. Recalling some encounter—the way F. cupped his hands around my rib cage to lift me in the pas de deux from *Les Sylphides*, for example, or the first time I felt his cane across my inner thigh—I feel branded by the gesture still, as if F.'s fingerprints will be on my body forever. Sometimes I even remember choreography. I look at myself in the mirror—even now—and suddenly I want to try an arabesque or some familiar *chaîné* turns; or I suddenly remember some lyrical, sweeping choreography that F. gave us to dance in class. So I mark these little dances for myself, my body not forgetting them and the music humming softly in my memory. It seems to me now that F. all along had been giving me not only ballet classes but transfusions, changing the very quality and temperature of my blood.

Some might think that I tell my story of F. so that I will never have to tell it again; so that there will be finality, closure. But no; writing is not catharsis: I will recall F. over and over, rehearse my stories about F. again and again; I won't "get beyond" them or transcend them or assimilate them into my now-very-ordinary real life. Sometimes I lie in bed at night, in the dark, still fascinated, telling these stories over and over to myself, reliving them. I have no wish to revise them, either the stories themselves or the memories. My secret theater is not going to fade.

Coda

Nor do I want to apportion blame. I am not trying to save some other little girl from a sadistic ballet master, or warn parents to keep their daughters away from ballet class. Perhaps the rigor and discipline, the self-mortification and the rhapsodic ambition I experienced are exactly what a girl needs to become "a great dancer"; perhaps F. was right all along, and it was I who failed in my vocation and not F. who betrayed me. When I remember whirling on F., after the final stroke of his cane for that forbidden cigarette, I still remember the tears in my eyes, and I can see myself at thirteen, what I must have looked like then, whipped and glowing, still defiant, about to cry. I never allowed myself to cry in front of him then, and I don't cry about him now, but I still remember everything about him. And I still adore him.

When I left F.—when I was expelled—I didn't mourn for him, I didn't grieve. But I do now. Beyond reason, I still long for and miss F., every tender, sardonic gesture of his, every outburst of whistling, every secret meeting in his room. I think that I tell these stories about F. so that I can dwell on them forever: I can keep him with me as my long-ago lover, the man who first taught me about love and risk and grief. This book is my elegy for him.